F. R. Oliphant

Notes of a Pilgrimage to Jerusalem and the Holy Land

F. R. Oliphant

Notes of a Pilgrimage to Jerusalem and the Holy Land

ISBN/EAN: 9783337281021

Printed in Europe, USA, Canada, Australia, Japan

Cover: Foto ©Andreas Hilbeck / pixelio.de

More available books at **www.hansebooks.com**

NOTES

OF A

PILGRIMAGE TO JERUSALEM AND THE HOLY LAND

BY

F. R. OLIPHANT, B.A.

WILLIAM BLACKWOOD AND SONS
EDINBURGH AND LONDON
MDCCCXCI

THE bulk of these sketches first appeared in a series of letters to the 'Spectator' in the summer of 1890. They have now been considerably enlarged, and the first and last chapters have been added, the former being chiefly intended to give some guidance to people purposing to visit the Holy Land, to whom some homely details of direct information such as are not usually vouchsafed by guide-books may not be unwelcome.

CONTENTS.

-

NOTES OF A PILGRIMAGE.

I.

INTRODUCTORY AND CHIEFLY PRACTICAL.

IN these prosaic days there is no very great degree of hardship involved in the notion of a pilgrimage to Jerusalem, at least for a pilgrim who does not think it necessary to gratuitously increase the hardships of the journey, and who is able, more or less, to pay his way. Still, being an unadventurous person, I will admit to having felt a certain natural shrinking from an expedition which looked so tremendous on the map; and imagining that there may be some future visitors equally timorous, I think it as well to put down a few facts which may

A

reassure them at least, and be of some use in
foreshadowing what they are to expect when
they arrive in the Holy Land. To begin with,
it is hardly necessary to say that the traveller
in Palestine has no longer to encounter the
dangers which are so delightful to read of in
the fascinating pages of 'Eothen,' and must
be so very disagreeable to encounter in reality,
unless he wilfully goes out of his way to look
for them.   There are still brigands in the mountains of Moab, who live near enough to civilisation to get an additional touch of roguery over
and above their natural predatory habits, who
would be delighted to oblige any gentleman who
has a fancy to go through the interesting experience of being robbed ; inquirers of this class are,
however, advised to travel with a very small
train, for fear of frightening robbers away.   It
is usual to amuse travellers on their way to the
Dead Sea with tales of possible Bedouin descents,
and dragomans are always careful to make very
ostentatious display of weapons on this expedition ; I was even taken to task myself at
Jericho — naturally by the last arrival from
Europe—for openly wearing a gold watch-chain,

which might excite the cupidity of neighbouring hordes, and bring destruction upon all of us. The traveller need take no account of such silly stories; danger there may be for those who go off the beaten track, but no inexperienced person should do this without a perfectly reliable drago-man. I am, of course, not writing for those who have a real knowledge of the country.

With regard to the means of getting to Palestine, the most usual route is that by Brindisi, from which the Austrian Lloyd steamers go once a-week to Alexandria, Port Said, Jaffa, &c., and the P. & O. ships weekly for Port Said, and fortnightly for Alexandria. The journey from Brindisi to Alexandria occupies about three days. A pleasant little tour in Egypt can be made in the few days elapsing between the arrival of one steamer at Alexandria and the starting of the next one from Port Said. This will give time for a glance at Cairo, the Pyramids of Gizeh—which are disappointing,—and the Sphinx—which is not. Of course, it is by no means fair to Egypt to try and see it in this way; but it is hardly a chance to be missed, and as there is no time to make one's way as

far as the greatest wonders of the land, this
flying visit does something to get the traveller
into tune for the sights he is to see—that is,
if the East is unfamiliar to him—and is hardly
sufficient to blunt his appetite. It was Thackeray's opinion that the most complete appre-
ciation of the East would be obtained by the
traveller who just got a sight of one thoroughly
Eastern town, and then at once turned his face
homewards and fled before he had time to lose
his first illusions on the subject. With this
theory I do not in the least agree. Though
beginning with a trifle like Cairo, I have found
the wonders I had expected to see, growing
greater and greater till they culminated at Damascus, where our voyage ended. Still, there is
certainly a great deal in the first impressions:
the first sight of an Eastern city, where one begins
to realise that there actually are regions where
the population, as a body, are opposed to the
wearing of conventional coats and trousers;
the first Arab mud village; the first string of
camels—above all, the first entry into a mosque
—are things not to be forgotten. There is a
faint glamour of the ' Arabian Nights ' even about

poor prosaic Alexandria—in its present fallen condition, a city about as interesting as Marseilles. The first ragged fellow one meets with, the extraordinary patchwork garment which serves him for a cloak only hanging together by some miracle of art, might serve for Hassan Alhabbal; he looks quite equal to making his fortune out of a lump of lead, if he only thought it worth his while to take the trouble. The old woman hobbling along in her blue cloak on the other side of the road, might be the very person who tried to lure the barber's brother to his death; while the two blind men feeling their way along together, with their boy in front to guide them, remind one of another member of that ill-starred family. At Cairo, of course, the illusion is greater: in spite of all the modern Europeanism of the place, in spite of the crowds of English travellers like ourselves—who, we are agreed, had much better have stayed at home—loafing about the entrances to the hotels, in spite of Tommy Atkins pacing up and down with his rifle over his shoulder, and the wives of Tommy Atkins's commanders generally pervading the atmosphere in carriages or on donkeys,

we see in the bazaars the really Eastern character of our surroundings. The chief question
that presented itself to our minds was, where
on earth these hordes of people could have come
from. I have seen immense crowds before on
great occasions in Europe; but such an unceasing stream, coming and going in every possible
direction, whichever way one turns, was a thing
not yet dreamed of in my philosophy. And
where, in the name of goodness, if the whole
of Egypt were roofed in, were they to be
housed? Subsequent experience of other Eastern cities has shown me that this swarming of
human creatures is not a characteristic of Egypt
alone, but it was certainly in this first view that
it made the most impression.

I have never been able to understand the
great enthusiasm into which some English
writers have worked themselves regarding the
religion of Islam; and it was consequently less
with any absolute feeling of reverence than with
a desire not to appear irreverent, that I entered
the Mosque of Sultan Hassan under the guidance of a pious Mohammedan dragoman, —
whose faith, I imagine, was greater than his

works, for his mysterious habit of returning alone to the shops where I had just made purchases was, to say the least of it, suspicious. But having already covered my infidel boots with good Moslem slippers, in obedience to Mohammedan prejudices, the involuntary feeling of veneration inspired by the place made me take my hat off also.   There is something to my mind strangely impressive about these Mohammedan churches.   There is none of the religious upholstery with which our places of worship are encumbered.   A large niche (*mihrab*) in the wall at one end to indicate the direction of Mecca—a great pulpit or canopied chair (*mimbar*) with a stair leading to it, from which passages from the Koran are occasionally read to the faithful—a small stone terrace or platform raised upon short columns for a similar purpose—and a profusion of lamps, make up the furniture of the mosque. Outside is a cool pleasant court, with a fountain in the centre where the necessary ablutions are performed, and where also passers-by may come in to rest and refresh themselves, and will seldom go away without a prayer or a holy thought. The mosque itself is, except on rare occasions, a

place for private prayer, or for the united devotions of a few who are gathered together by
chance, or have come in a body for the purpose.
Such a party we found in the Citadel Mosque
kneeling in a row, with one of their number,
probably more learned in the necessary prayers,
in front of them to lead. The spectacle of this
little group, muttering together and bowing their
heads in concert, or turning them from side to
side to the two angels who stand on either hand
of every man to record, one his good and the
other his bad actions, gave an added solemnity
to the great, cold, silent hall. It was most
truly a house of prayer—one was inclined to say,
the house of God. Yet when one among us
spoke of it as a place where one might say one's
own prayers, there was a strange repugnance to
the idea, which yet I cannot well explain. There
is something natural in the disgust one feels at
seeing a Christian church turned into a mosque,
with all its sacred emblems forcibly erased, or
even one that is erected upon a spot which
has any sacred associations with our own
faith ; but it is hard to see any reason why we
should not kneel in the same house of prayer

with pious men who worship the same God, because they include in their devotions the names of other men whom they regard with an excessive veneration. But man is an animal little governed by reason.

A day's journey brings one from Cairo to Port Said, half-way by railway to Ismailia and half-way by small steamer up the Suez Canal. From Port Said four lines of steamers go to Palestine —the Austrian Lloyd, the Messageries, a Russian company, and the Egyptian Khedivich mail-steamers. I believe, though I do not personally know, that the last named are a rather inferior class of ships; the French, Austrian, and Russian are equally good, though at some seasons, especially a short time before Easter, they are most inconveniently crowded. We ourselves had to give up all hopes of the Austrian Lloyd, and thought ourselves lucky to secure sleeping-room in the saloon of the Russian steamer which started a day later. I cannot wish my worst enemy a harder fate than to spend two days at Port Said, though it was certainly comfortable to have a bed—and even a bedroom—for the second night. The first had to be got through on chairs or tables, or in cupboards or anything that offered. Some people say that Egypt is so delightful a place that one feels it difficult to leave it. We certainly found the process of leaving a most troublesome one.

The journey to Jaffa only takes one night, but there is always the pleasing prospect, during bad weather, that it may be found impossible to land passengers at Jaffa: all may consequently have to be taken on to Beyrout. I never heard of an instance myself, but it is said to happen occasionally; those who are afraid of such consequences had better decide at once to go on to Beyrout, which is an excellent starting-place for the journey through Palestine, though not in Palestine itself. To us the difficulties of the landing at Jaffa appeared to have been exaggerated. There are certainly some very nasty reefs close to the shore; but the channel of entrance to the harbour is fairly wide, and easily managed in all but really stormy weather. It is said to have been here that Perseus turned the sea-monster, who was about to devour Andromeda, into stone, and the reefs may well be supposed to be some portions of his petrified carcass.   Considering the trouble they have caused since his time, one is inclined to doubt whether Perseus was justified in treating a harmless necessary monster in such a manner.

Once on shore, after a little troublesome waiting in the custom-house till the authorities have settled the amount of bribe required for letting you pass freely, the traveller will probably stumble through the dirty streets of Jaffa till he reaches Mr Hardeck's hotel on the outskirts of the town.   It may not be out of place here to mention what kind of hotel accommodation is to be found in the country we are speaking of.   There are excellent hotels at Jerusalem, Damascus, and Beyrout ; my own experience at the last-named place was not a favourable one, but that was the result of arriving late at night in a crowded season. . We had to be packed off to a sort of *succursale,* which, though a fine old Syrian house, was otherwise undesirable, the cookery being wretched and the wine atrocious.   But I believe the first-class hotels are good.   The Grand New Hotel at Jerusalem, and the Victoria at Damascus, I can heartily recommend from personal experience.

There are also hotels of a sort at Jaffa, Ramleh, Jericho, Haifa, Nazareth, Storah, and, I believe, Baalbek. Those at Jaffa, Haifa, and Ramleh are kept by members of the German Society of the Temple, which fact is in itself—as every one who knows Palestine will agree—a guarantee for cleanliness, honesty, and an eager desire to do everything that is possible for strangers of all kinds, whether guests staying in the hotel or not. That at Jericho is a nice little place, well conducted, though perhaps a little primitive in its arrangements. One does not expect much more than a bivouac at Jericho, and from that point of view the hotel is luxurious.[1]   At Storah, in the great plain of the Bukeia, between the Lebanon and Anti-Lebanon ranges, there is now, I believe, a good hotel : though when we were there, the accommodation was of a very primitive nature.

Where there are no regular houses of entertainment, it is always possible to put up at

[1] Since I was in Palestine, I believe some progress has been made in regard to hotel accommodation ; but as this has chiefly consisted in starting opposition establishments where there was already a hotel existing, I have not thought it necessary to alter what I had written.

a monastery; but most travellers in the more rural parts of Palestine will prefer to live in their own tents: this can be made a most luxurious form of life. The places I have mentioned are chiefly on the outskirts of the country in which the greatest points of interest lie. Some visitors prefer to take to tent-life at once from their first landing at Jaffa; but the greater number keep to the more civilised habits as far as Jerusalem at least, and only begin their camping life when they make their first move northwards. There is at least no trouble with the weather in well-built stone houses. For a couple of days at Jericho the hotel there is a great convenience, and most travellers will be content to give up their tents at Damascus and return to ordinary life. The hotels, in fact, are to be found in the parts of Palestine where it is possible without extreme discomfort to travel in carriages of some kind, as well as in the sea-coast towns where the great steamers call.

Carriages as means of conveyance can only be used in a few localities. There is an excellent carriage-road from Beyrout to Damascus, and there are passable specimens between Jaffa and

Jerusalem, and between Jerusalem and Bethany
and Bethlehem. It is said to be possible to
drive on beyond Bethlehem to Hebron, but it is
certainly in the highest degree unadvisable.
Driving is also possible at a very slow pace
and with great discomfort along the coast from
Jaffa to Haifa. In the neighbourhood of the
latter place the native roads have been much
improved by the efforts of the German settlers,
who also keep up a regular communication with
Nazareth by waggon, for goods at least. Passengers would find the journey rather fatiguing, as the road still leaves much to be desired,
and the conveyances are of the rudest kind.
The German waggoners had to fight their way
against native marauders at first; but there
is very rarely any trouble of this kind now,
brigandage in this district having been practically extinguished, as half the inhabitants are
awed by the honesty of their German neighbours, and the other half are frightened by their
courage. It is most advisable not to try any
travelling by carriage between Jerusalem and
Damascus, but the journey connecting either of
these places with the coast is most conveniently

done in this manner.   The best plan at the commencement of the journey is to rest for a while at Jaffa and lunch there, driving on in the afternoon to Ramleh, some fifteen miles away, where there is a fine Crusaders' church, now a mosque, a curious old tower, and a rather makeshift hotel.   Here will be found also the first instance of one of the saddest sights in Palestine, the wretched groups of lepers who sit and beg by the roadside ; few travellers will pass without giving some trifling alms to the sufferers from this awful affliction.   The remainder of the journey to Jerusalem, about twenty-five miles further, can be accomplished with great ease the next day.   The road is not of any particular interest, except for the picturesque gorge which bears the name of Ali, the Prophet's son-in-law, and the village of Abu Gosh,—sometimes identified with Kirjath-jearim,—where there are the remains of a fine church of the crusading times.

For the journey through Palestine, riding is almost the only possible mode of progression. Care should be taken as to the selection of horses, upon the quality of which the speed and comfort of the journey naturally depend.   The

Cook agency—and I have no doubt that of Mr
Gaze also—can generally be relied on to supply
sufficiently good horses, but a little personal
superintendence never does any harm.   For
those who dislike this mode of conveyance,
the only resource for the long journeys across
country is that of a mule-palanquin, a kind of
wooden box, something like a sedan-chair, supported on two long poles, the ends of which are
borne by one mule in front and another behind.
Travelling in this manner is exceedingly uncomfortable, especially in hilly country, as the
mules are unable to take advantage of the zig-
zag paths, owing to the difficulty of turning,
and have to go straight up and straight down.
Still it is a way in which people who are incap-
able of riding can visit practically every spot of
interest in Palestine.   I only suggest it for cases
of physical incapability, as no knowledge of
horsemanship is required for a hundred miles'
journey on the back of such sedate and peaceable animals as are usually provided for tourists.

The manner of travelling through the country
will be new to the great majority of visitors.
Great care should be taken in the selection of

a dragoman. To the inexperienced tourist, ignorant of Eastern languages and Eastern ways generally, the dragoman is a kind of impersonation
of Providence, to whom he must look for the
regulation of all his worldly affairs. With a
thoroughly qualified person to fill this important post, the traveller enjoys a happy freedom
from all responsibility, with a general sense
that every arrangement is made for him very
much better than he could do it himself. The
choice, however, is naturally difficult for the
inexperienced, for whom the safest plan is probably to put themselves at once into the hands
of Messrs Cook. There are independent dragomans who are as good as can be desired, but
it is not always easy to find the best of them :
it is at least a very unsafe course to select the
most plausible, as, in the absence of any information on the subject, one is very apt to do.
There are also other agencies besides that of
Messrs Cook, but I only speak of things of
which I have personal knowledge. We were,
I believe, very exceptionally fortunate in secur-
ing the services of Mr David Jamal, of whose
qualifications it is difficult to speak too highly.

B

An admirable manager of all things under his care, an excellent chief for the numerous retinue which is necessary even for the smallest party, an intelligent guide for all that is worth seeing, and a pleasant, and never intrusive companion,—I am not sure whether it may not appear a lower kind of commendation to speak of his remarkable talent for bargaining, which stood us in such good stead in Damascus and Constantinople. Mr Jamal is one of the dragomans in the employment of Messrs Cook.

The engagement of the subordinate servants can safely be left to the dragoman. A cook is of the first necessity, a butler, with probably an assistant to wait at table, a groom or two, and a number of muleteers, varying according to the amount of luggage, will make up the train required. With regard to luggage, I do not believe there is any article, of whatever weight and size, which could not be conveyed on a mule's back; but for obvious reasons of convenience and economy—not to mention cruelty to animals—it is desirable to have as small and, I may add, as strong articles of baggage as is reasonably possible. Stores of all kinds are easily procurable at Jerusalem or any of the principal towns; they are not, however, easily renewed on the way, and one of the most objectionable features of such a journey is usually the condition of staleness to which the bread is reduced after the first two or three days. Very fair light wine of the country can be bought at Jerusalem, both red and white : the red carries best. It is the fashion with English travellers to declare that the Jerusalem wine is undrinkable,—as indeed what country is there where the genial Englishman does not pronounce the native wine too bad for his uneducated palate ?—but it is really by no means bad. The Lebanon wine is also good, when it is good ; Jaffa wine is inferior, and that of Safed a trifle less disagreeable than Dead Sea water.

A word about languages may not be out of place. A knowledge of Arabic would be of immense value in making the traveller independent ; but only comparatively few visitors to the Holy Land usually possess this accomplishment. With a competent dragoman, it is quite possible to see everything in the Holy Land without knowing a word of any language but English. European languages, however, are useful. French is spoken generally in Beyrout,

and many of the officials and the richer merchants in all parts of Syria can speak it; Italian
is understood in most Levantine coast towns,
and is also useful in speaking to Latin monks,
many of whom are Italians: many also are
Spaniards. German is of advantage for the
German Society of the Temple—though many
of them speak English—and for German-speaking
Jews. Modern Greek might also be useful with
Greek priests, but is hardly more generally known
among us than Arabic.

The line of route chosen by the traveller on
leaving Jerusalem will depend chiefly upon the
time at his disposal. The journey I am about
to speak of myself was undertaken with certain
particular objects, which made us stay longer
than is usual at certain places, and miss
out altogether some others which are well
worth visiting, but for which we had no time
left. Baalbek, which the traveller under ordinary circumstances should certainly not omit,
unfortunately fell in the latter category. The
usual route goes straight northwards from Jerusalem by Nablous (the ancient Shechem) and
Samaria to Jezreel (the modern Zerin) and

Nazareth, from which point travellers generally proceed in the manner described below. By the very easiest stages, Nazareth should be reached on the fourth day after leaving Jerusalem, and Damascus about a week later, by the ordinary route as I have given it. Mount Carmel is, however, entirely left out of this route, which is, undoubtedly, a pity. Those who wish to include it may, however, make a special expedition from Nazareth for the purpose: it could easily be done in three days extra, and would prove of great interest. To go as we did, from Jaffa to Haifa by sea, is to leave out Nablous and all the famous scenes of Old Testament history which lie between Jerusalem and the great plain of Esdraelon, in the country of the children of Joseph. A course strongly recommended by some is to strike off from Nablous to Beisan (the ancient Bethshean), and from thence proceed straight to Tiberias, which can be reached in two days' journey, or leave the usual route at Jenin in the plain of Esdraelon, and travel straight on by Nain and Mount Tabor. The Lake of Tiberias having been seen, the traveller would now turn backwards to Nazareth (one day), and thence over Mount Carmel to Haifa (two days), and finally to Beyrout along the coast by Acre, Tyre, and Sidon, a profoundly interesting route, which could be accomplished in four days more, allowing for easy travelling and time to view the wonders of these famous cities. The coast road by Tyre has recently been much improved. Beyrout would thus be reached in twelve days at most from Jerusalem, or little more than the time which would be occupied by the ordinary route to Damascus. From Beyrout to Damascus is a day's journey in a carriage, over a splendid road; on horseback the time would be considerably longer. From Damascus, the Baalbek expedition can be made on horseback, going on from Baalbek by Storah to Beyrout, instead of returning to Damascus. Beyrout should be reached on the sixth day, allowing one whole day at Baalbek.[1]

The time of arrival at Beyrout is a matter of importance, by which most movements are regulated for those who begin their journey

[1] It is now possible to reach Baalbek by carriage from Storah.

from the south.   The steamers only call at Beyrout every fortnight, so that arrangements have to be made to arrive there at a suitable time.   The return is generally made by Austrian Lloyd, Messageries, or Russian steamer to Smyrna, from which it is equally easy to cross to Athens or go on to Constantinople.   The Austrian line goes by Cyprus, Rhodes, and the coast of Asia Minor, the Russian varies the route by following the coast the whole way, while the Messageries steamers do a little of both.   The voyage between the western coast of Asia Minor and the islands of Rhodes, Cos, Samos, Chios, and Lesbos is extremely beautiful, and full of historical interest. Of course it stands to reason that it is equally possible to reach Palestine from this side and go back by Egypt, though this is not the usual custom ; and many people even, who come by Egypt, prefer to start on their journey through Palestine from Beyrout.   It is hardly necessary to say that the routes I have mentioned will take, in almost every case, the same time, and have the same interest from whichever end the start is made.   For my own part, I should recommend beginning with Jerusalem.

II.

JERUSALEM : THE HOLY SEPULCHRE.

IT appears to be the custom to say that Jerusalem is disappointing. As my own experience leads me to a directly contrary conclusion, I must assume that this is due to the fact that the first aspect of the city is not so impressive as one would expect, or perhaps wish it to be. Wherein appears a fresh instance of the good fortune which continually befriended me. Our journey, being only from Ramleh, was certainly not a very formidable one ; but still, many hours' jolting in a cramped position over what, being as yet ignorant of Palestine, we considered an indifferent road, will produce fatigue, and may account for the otherwise disgraceful fact that, on arriving in sight of Jerusalem, I was asleep. Being abruptly roused from slumber by well-meaning friends, I had not composed my feelings into a fitting frame of mind to look at any view till I found myself standing on the terrace of the Mediterranean Hotel, with all Jerusalem before me. I should recommend other travellers to adopt something of the same plan; the preliminaries need not be exactly similar.

The view that I speak of embraced almost all that is of real interest in Jerusalem. Almost at our feet lay the Pool of Hezekiah, a rather turbid-looking piece of water, built in on all sides, the houses running sheer down into the water without any kind of path or bank between. Beyond this came the most conspicuous object, the Church of the Holy Sepulchre, with its two domes and the old square roofless tower of the belfry, backed by low green hills, one of them being Mount Scopus, from which Titus looked down of old on the beautiful city which he was to destroy. Farther away to the right comes the great open space of the Haram-esh-Sherif, the site of Solomon's Temple, with the mosques of Omar and El Aksa. The Mohammedan feast of Moses is held at the same time as the Christian Easter, and the broad expanse of greensward

which occupies the place of the Court of the
Gentiles was dotted with picturesque figures of
pious Moslems, who spend their whole existence
for the time within the precincts of the mosque.
As a background for the Mosque of Omar, we
have the Mount of Olives, somewhat spoiled by
the hideous steeple erected on the top by a
pious Russian lady. The rest of the view is
chiefly made up by an infinity of tiny domes,
which are merely the roofs of ordinary houses,
interspersed with a few minarets—very few for
a city of the size of Jerusalem—some larger
domes of churches and synagogues, and in one
or two places a little foliage. The moderate
extent of the city contributes to give it an air of
greater completeness and uniformity. Beyond
the limits of the last wall, modern improvement
has done its ugliest to spoil the landscape; but
within there is fortunately little room for new
buildings, and the long line of domes and terraces
stretches away unbroken except by the small
dark clefts that mark here and there the intervention of one of the narrow, winding streets.
The mouth of one of the most frequented lay
just below us, where the street of David de-

bouches on the open place in front of the citadel. It was, like most Eastern streets, a seething mass of humanity, their garments in every conceivable variety of shape and colour,—sober, Christian Syrians in a kind of semi-European attire, with their lower extremities encased in a curious baggy garment, half pantaloons, half petticoat; Jews with shaven heads, all but the two long ringlets in front, and battered soft black hats—except in this respect, they are often magnificently dressed; wild-looking Bedouins in their striped burnouses, from the further shores of the Dead Sea or the desert of the South; and here and there, to increase the variety of the picture, some large-limbed Russian peasant-pilgrim, in the same long caftan, fur cap, and high boots that he wears at home, shouldering his way through the crowd to make some purchase for his scanty evening meal. We had little to find fault with in our first sight of Jerusalem.

A great proportion of this motley crowd are probably attracted here by religious motives—either their own or those of others. For the most pious pilgrims must eat and drink, and even for those who have free quarters at the

Greek, Latin, or Armenian monasteries, food of some kind must be obtained and paid for by some one. Then, of course, among the Christians there is a lavish trade in rosaries, sacred pictures, and the like, by which many worthy persons live and prosper. The motives of this latter class can only be regarded as very indirectly pious. But the quantity of people who have really come to settle here with no other motives than those of religious enthusiasm and love for the holy places of their creed, without any professional inducements or the least touch of ecclesiasticism, is astounding to the inhabitant of a respectable Christian country, where men of business go to church on Sundays and idle people on other days also. These religious motives extend to several creeds, each of which has its special objects of veneration, and each of which also naturally regards the other sects as intruders. The times are long gone by when the Psalmist could describe Jerusalem as a city which was at unity with itself. Nowadays it is a place of much contention and jealousy, where the Latin Christian hates his Greek brother, and the Greek Catholic

detests the Latin. The Mohammedan holds
both the great divisions of Christianity in
equal abhorrence, and all three combine in
their loathing for the Jew. The last named
profess perhaps the most enthusiastic feeling
for Jerusalem, arising probably from the fact
that to them the city is sacred for its own
sake, apart from any especial hallowed spot
to which importance is given by particular
incident. Jerusalem itself is the object of the
religious aspirations of the Jew. Perhaps a
particular sanctity may be atttached to the
site of the Temple, but I greatly doubt whether
any Jew is allowed to penetrate within the
sacred enclosure of the Noble Sanctuary. The
one spot to which they gather is outside the
Temple, beneath the great stones of the outer
wall, where wealthy merchants, in gorgeous
robes of silk and velvet, and thrifty small shop-
keepers, in patched and ragged garments of every
description, unite in their strange ceremony of
wailing, swaying their bodies from side to side,
or pressing their foreheads against the wall, as
they mutter over Jeremiah's words of bitter
lamentation over the fall of Zion. " Her gates

are sunk into the ground; he hath destroyed
and broken her bars: her king and her princes
are among the Gentiles: the law is no more;
her prophets also find no vision from the Lord.
The elders of the daughter of Zion sit upon the
ground, and keep silence: they have cast up
dust upon their heads; they have girded themselves with sackcloth: the virgins of Jerusalem
hang down their heads to the ground." How
bitterly real these sad words must be as they
are read to-day by those to whom this terrible
legacy of sorrow and subjection has been left!
There is a dignity of grief about the custom
that makes one pass over many details that
seem petty, and even absurd, to the stranger.

To us the city is holy also—without, of
course, the distinct national feeling which in-
tensifies the devotion of the Jew—but in a
higher and broader sense, as the scene where
God humbled Himself to put on human form,
and even consented to endure death in the
most degrading form known to that age, the
death appointed for pirates, runaway slaves,
and the refuse of mankind. But the memory
of the last and greatest scenes of His life ties

us down more than the Jews to particular spots
which are difficult to realise in the midst of the
crowded busy city, most difficult of all when
it is the business of devotion which is being
carried on. The scenes of the Passion are
all marked out with the utmost care for our
guidance, perhaps with too much care not to
detract from the sense of reality. Our guide
was as certain of the identity of the places
he pointed out as more learned critics may
be that the traditions connected with them
rest upon no authority whatever. The difference of sites, however, cannot be very material,
it seemed to us, at least while we were in the
open air. Let us take that Turkish barrack to
stand on the site of Pilate's Judgment-hall, and
the arch adjoining the Convent of the Sisters
of Zion to mark the spot where our Lord was
brought forth to the multitude.

Most of us will follow from thence with
reverent hearts the long line of the Via Dolorosa all the way to the Church of the Holy
Sepulchre. We are in no mood for carping at
the harmless traditions that have grown up
around the great theme of sacred story; we

find little difficulty in believing that it was
at that corner at the bottom of the valley, that
the soldiers caught sight of Simon of Cyrene
" coming out of the country," and forced him to
help in carrying the cross.   It may well have
been that some pious woman came out at the
very spot where the house of St Veronica is
pointed out to us, to soothe and soften the
sufferings of our Lord as He dragged His way
up that weary ascent; nor do we smile at the
innocent absurdity which fixes a site even for
the houses of Dives and Lazarus.   But when
we arrive at last at the very spot where the
great tragedy was enacted, we begin to lose the
feeling of reality that has brought us through all
the preceding scenes.   It is hard for a man to
stand in that great church, or rather amalga-
mation of churches, with all its garish decorations, surrounded by all the appurtenances of
religious pageantry, Greek or Roman, and say to
himself: " This is the hill where our Saviour
was brought out to die; here actually stood the
cross on which He was bound, and there the
sepulchre where His body was laid, and from
which He rose again."   We cannot help a dis-

tinct revulsion of feeling, an idea that this is not what we have come out to see. The thought of tracing the course of that last procession is given up, as we find each sacred spot encumbered with all the paraphernalia of devotion, distracting the eye, and entirely obliterating all sense of locality.

The Church of the Holy Sepulchre is a large and imposing building, which bears strong testimony in every corner to the piety of the faithful who erected and adorned it. It seemed to us that they were only too ready to do their inartistic best to beautify the house of the Lord. The entry is characteristically marked by a divan, on which the Turkish guardians of the edifice lounge and smoke, and float their infidel minds in oceans of coffee. The first spot which is held in any great veneration is marked by a great reddish block of marble, supposed by innocent pilgrims to be the stone on which our Lord's body was laid during the funeral ceremonies of anointing. As a point of fact, many stones are known to have succeeded each other in this office. Passing beyond this, we come to the great rotunda, which is built round what is

C

supposed to be the actual burying-place of our
Lord. The sepulchre itself is enclosed within
a small chapel, which remains, in spite of the
numerous lamps which contending sects keep
perpetually burning there, in a state of almost
unbroken darkness : especially about the time of
Easter, when our visit was made, and when
great numbers of pilgrims are always crowding
in, it is very difficult to distinguish anything at
all here. The rotunda is open to Christians of
all sects ; but the Church of the Resurrection,
opening out of it, and next in importance, is the
property of the Greek Catholics. On the other
hand, the chapels connected with the supposed
site of Calvary—on a higher level in the same
building — belong chiefly to the Latins. All
kinds of different sects have little *pieds-à-terre*
in the great building, and the ignorant visitor is
often not a little confused by the various ways
in which different Churches combine or oppose
each other in their veneration for the sacred
spots. For instance, of the forty-three lamps
which burn above the Holy Sepulchre, the
Greek, Latin, and Armenian communities own
thirteen each, the remaining four belonging to

the Copts. Still more intricate is the case of the chapel of St Helena, which is the property of the Abyssinian Church, who let it for religious purposes to the Armenians. But this is nothing to the confusion, worse confounded, which comes upon the pilgrim who tries to follow out the various incidents of the great tragedy which are here commemorated. It is true that numberless authentic sites are pointed out to us. In this place, we are told, our Lord was mocked, here He was scourged, here the soldiers cast lots for His garment; but hurrying round from one dark chapel to another only increases our confusion. We cannot help wishing that the devotion of ages had shown itself in some less practical way than that of building churches over the holy places, and decorating them to an unlimited extent when erected. Of course this is a most improper view of the case. It was the most natural and fitting way to testify reverence for these holy places; it has, no doubt, done good service in marking the spots and keeping them from pollution; above all, it is a great boon to the thousands of pilgrims who come here with less

artificial ideas on the subject,—witness the kind
of wondering awed delight with which that little
band of Russian peasants comes upon one after
another of these relics of the day of salvation,—
but to me it was almost a comfort that recent
discoveries have made it possible that the sites
of the Crucifixion and burial were not here at
all. A few days before the suggestion had
seemed almost impious, but now I felt an un-
reasonable conviction of its correctness. I had
rather have the faith of the Russians, but as a
pis aller I could take refuge with the Palestine
Exploration Society.

The first doubt thrown upon the authenticity
of the recognised sites of Golgotha and of the
Holy Sepulchre, came from the supposition that
these must have been within the wall of the
city as then standing. I believe this question
is not yet settled to the satisfaction of all; but
most of the investigations carried on by the
able workers for the Palestine Exploration Fund
seem to represent them as being within the walls.
There can be no doubt whatever that the place
set apart for such an unclean purpose as the
execution of criminals must have been outside.

Few other indications of its site can be gathered ;
but we know it to have been near a garden
where there was a sepulchre, and this sepulchre
would most probably be on the north side of the
city, as the great cemetery of Jewish times lay
on that side, by the great road which ran northwards through the whole of Palestine.   Starting
with these slight directions, Colonel Conder hit
upon what is now very generally accepted as the
real place of the Crucifixion.

It is a round green hill just outside the
Damascus Gate, chiefly remarkable till recent
days for the grotto on its southern side, where,
according to tradition, Jeremiah wrote the
Lamentations.   On the summit, a number of
Mohammedan tombs are scattered about, but
otherwise the hill is left quite free ; indeed, I
believe it has now been bought by a well-known
German resident in Jerusalem, for the express
purpose of preventing any building upon it.

It is the traditionary place of the stoning of
St Stephen to the Christians of Jerusalem, and
the Jews, who care little for St Stephen, yet
describe it themselves as " the place of stoning,"
a spot set apart for executions from very ancient

times, and mentioned as such in rabbinical writings.   Certainly it is outside the walls, as Calvary was—of that we have ocular demonstration from the great rock-foundations which have been laid bare here and there under the present walls.   Also, if there be anything in the name of Golgotha implying more than a general connection with death, by going a little way down the road between the walls and the hill, we have ocular demonstration of the striking resemblance this little hill bears to a skull.   I was tempted to decide in its favour chiefly by sentimental reasons.   If it be the right spot, it has not changed its appearance, except for the tombs upon it, since the three crosses were planted on its summit.   Few people come there: I have seen no one but a few Mohammedan women, going through some ceremonies of mourning at the tombs in a very casual, not to say jovial, manner; and once a little group of children, to whom an old man was reciting the story of Joseph being sold by his brethren and carried away into Egypt.   It is easier, at least, to dream in that quiet spot, to reconstruct in one's own mind all the details of that terrible day, than it is in the great church, with its profusion of shrines and altars, of monster candles and bad pictures, and extravagant if not tawdry ornament.

It is, however, only with painful reluctance that I can bring myself to abandon the recognised Via Dolorosa. Yet if Colonel Conder's theories be correct, only a small portion can have been in the actual line of the procession. At the foot of the hill by the broken column, where Simon was called to bear the cross, they must have turned to the right instead of to the left, towards the Damascus Gate, on the site of which an ancient gate existed, very possibly from those times. Once beyond the gate, the place of execution would be straight before them. The way would in this case be shorter and less toilsome than that leading to the Church of the Holy Sepulchre. The words of the evangelists, however, do not seem to point to a long road. There are many other things, too, of course, which must be given up if the accepted site of the Sepulchre is not the genuine one. For myself, I grieve chiefly to think how hopelessly off the right track St Helena must have been, with all her treasured discoveries

mere illusions. I think of her sitting in the
chair that is pointed out in her chapel, watch-
ing her men at their work,—I picture her to
myself in the yellow drapery given her in a
picture of Tintoretto's in a small church at
Venice, on the further side of the Rialto, I
think, Santa Maria Mater Domini,—and all the
growing excitement as the explorations went on,
and the frantic enthusiasm when the crosses were
discovered. I can imagine even then cynical
courtiers remarking to each other that when a
pious (and probably generous) Empress under-
takes excavations with the avowed object of
finding certain crosses, crosses are pretty sure to
turn up somehow or other. It is hard to think
of so much pious enthusiasm being thrown away,
and of the good Empress exulting over what
she thought to be her great discoveries; one
might almost believe that she had been handed
over to some tricksy evil spirit with full licence
to cheat her and lead her astray. However, I
believe that certain historical critics maintain
that there is no evidence that St Helena ever
had anything to do with it, only that excavations
were made in the time of Constantine, and that

he built a magnificent church over what was
supposed to be the sepulchre of our Lord. In
which case, as I do not care three straws for
any illusion that Constantine may have been
led into, I should unhesitatingly give my vote
for Colonel Conder. At any rate, it would be a
comfort to think that it was not over the actual
tomb of our Lord that the miserable jugglery of
the "sacred fire" is perpetrated, nor around it
that the annual bear-fight takes place, which
precedes and accompanies that astounding ceremony.

III.

.

ONE of the earliest convictions impressed upon
the mind of the traveller to Palestine is that
the Turk is a nuisance. The gigantic absurdity,
to call it nothing more, of leaving all these holy
places, the centre of veneration to all Christen-
dom, in Mohammedan hands, produces a natural
feeling of irritation, which is constantly freshened
and revived by some vexatious regulation or
piece of official red-tapeism, causing the most
peaceable pilgrim to regret that the period of
holy wars is past, and consider seriously the advisability of preaching a crusade himself on his
return from the parts of the infidel. It is sufficient to talk with any resident who has ever
had any serious business with that hopeless
Government—especially those who are trying to

introduce any kind of progress or improvement in Palestine—to find a good solid foundation for this feeling against the Turkish rulers; the ordinary traveller is exasperated by their mere presence. Here we find, in the first place, the unspeakable Turk occupying for his own purposes the site of the Temple, and raising beautiful buildings thereupon for his own worship. This, we consider, is bad enough; but when he comes to celebrating his own religious festivals there, and consequently excluding all but Mohamme-dans from the whole area during the time that we are at Jerusalem, the enormity is still more remarkable. This is not even a coincidence. The benighted paynim does not want for worldly wisdom, and, having no confidence whatever in the doctrine of peace on earth and goodwill to-wards men, as understood by enthusiastic pil-grims, he has established a feast of his own, which attracts a sufficient number of Moham-medans to counterbalance the Christians. To these latter the whole of the Haram-esh-Sherif[1] is closed, and many poor pilgrims who cannot

[1] The Noble Sanctuary; the Arabic name for the Temple enclosure.

afford to stay long at Jerusalem are obliged to go away without having seen the place of the Temple, a very real hardship to some of them.

Being a little less pressed for time than some others, we were able to pay one visit to the Haram-esh-Sherif. The last of the pious Mohammedans had been packed off with much beating of drums, clashing of cymbals, and waving of banners, on their pilgrimage to the spot where it is extremely unlikely that Moses was buried, and in the whole of the enclosure there was scarcely a figure to be seen. We were not, however, suffered to enter without protectors, our body-guard consisting of the *cavasse* of the Consulate, a gentleman of ferocious aspect, with a gold-laced jacket and a curved scimitar, and an aged Turkish non-commissioned officer, who followed us about brandishing a huge pair of top-boots, in reality taken off from motives of piety, but apparently to be used as offensive weapons. Our time was very short; but I believe that if you cannot spend three weeks over the Temple, it is better to see it in half an hour. Certainly no subsequent visit can show anything to surpass the first view of the whole. We pass in by the beautiful judgment-hall, where the Cadi administered justice at the gate in times gone by, into a vast enclosure, some five hundred yards long, and at least half as wide, studded in all directions with countless little domes and cupolas. The central platform, roughly identified with the Court of the Jews, as the outer zone is with that of the Gentiles, is paved, but most of the rest remains as nature made it, and green grass and trees make a contrast with the white walls and the many-coloured domes. Some of these are merely canopies over the numerous fountains indispensable in a Mohammedan place of worship; others form a sheltered place for prayer, supplied with a *mihrab*, or niche in the direction of Mecca, to guide the devotions of the pious, or serve to mark some spot of particular sanctity; while the row of low domed buildings to the north of the central platform are even utilised as sleeping-rooms by devotees from a distance. Going up by a broad flight of low steps, topped by a single row of graceful arches, we come upon the gem of the whole, the exquisite Dome of the Rock itself. Certainly no one can accuse the Mohammedans of neglecting to make the house of God beautiful. It is true that this building was probably the work of Christian artists under Mohammedan orders; but this only shows that the early Arab conquerors had sufficient wisdom and piety to seek for their most holy shrine something which they could understand to be finer than their own rude architecture.

The Dome of the Rock, though by far the most important building of the central platform, is merely, like many of the others, a kind of shrine built over the most sacred of all the holy places. It is an octagonal building, measuring about twenty yards in every direction, built around the great flat rock to which so many traditions are attached. The exterior is richly, almost gaudily, decorated with coloured marbles and Damascus tiles, and the interior also has been made beautiful with mosaics and profuse decoration of every kind. But these have not the effect that we have deplored in the most sacred Christian shrine, of obstructing the view of the principal object of veneration, or even distracting the eye from it. The rock, which occupies the whole centre of the building, surrounded by a balustrade of painted wood, is plain to the sight even of a large concourse of people, and though the amount of light which penetrates through the stained glass of the windows is not exactly dazzling, it is at any rate a great advance upon the profound obscurity which conceals the Holy Sepulchre. Altogether, the idea that this shrine gives is that of a perfect composition, where, while the eye can find in every corner some beauty of detail to rest upon, the attention is naturally concentrated on the most important point. The admirable art with which the decoration is lavished on the background, while the rock is left in its bare simplicity as the centre of all, seems to me at least far more impressive than all the flummery of gold and silver lamps about the Holy Sepulchre.

I am speaking, of course, of the generally recognised Sepulchre. It is worth remembering, however, that the mosque in which we are standing was considered by no less an authority than the late James Fergusson to be the Church of the Resurrection built by Constantine over the actual tomb of our Lord, represented by the grotto underneath the stone. This idea has never been generally accepted, and has now probably ceased to have any adherents at all, but Mr Fergusson himself was never shaken in his belief. Certainly all probability seems against it, still it is strange to think that so great an authority on architecture should have made a mistake of three clear centuries as to the date of the building. What the rock actually does represent is not very certain. The Mussulmans, of course, have its history quite pat, and a very wonderful rock it must have been, according to them. Not only was it the scene of Abraham's proposed sacrifice of his son — in which story Christian and Jewish tradition appear to agree — but it is also connected with the personal history of Mohammed himself. Here the Prophet is known to have prayed, and from here he ascended to heaven on his wonderful mule " Alborak," after that sagacious animal had secured for itself a place in Paradise under threats of not allowing him to remount. The influence of the Sent of God was so powerful, that the rock was enabled to hold converse with him — as it did later with the Caliph Omar —

and even attempted to follow him in his aerial voyage,—a purpose which it might have achieved, but for the thoughtful action of the archangel Gabriel, who arrested it just in time. The marks of the angel's fingers are there to this day; so that this story at least must be true. Jewish tradition tends to see here the rock on which the ark rested, and consequently the Holy of Holies, which, however, is more usually placed at a point some way to the south-west, near the top of the stairs by which we approached. The theory that on this rock stood the altar of burnt-offerings is supported by the existence of a channel which might have served to let the blood run down into the cave below, and perhaps through the hollow which evidently exists under the round stone at its centre. Explorers have desired to make further researches by raising this stone; but though the necessary authorisation was obtained from Constantinople, the local authorities were immovable on the subject. The stone, they averred, formed the cover of the Well of the Evil Spirit; and, as they very reasonably argued, if it were removed, the Evil Spirit would get out, and might literally play the

D

devil with Jerusalem, a contingency against
which they, as responsible rulers, were bound to
provide. So the mystery is likely to remain
unsolved.

The central platform abounds in beautiful
little shrines, though none of them can be said
to come up to the masterpiece of which we have
spoken. It should be mentioned, by the way,
that the Dome of the Rock, believed by the
early Crusaders to be either the original Temple
of Solomon, or at least an exact copy, became
the model for the majority of churches belonging to the Order of the Templars, the Temple
Church in London being one instance. Among
the most striking of the smaller shrines is the
little Dome of the Chain, sometimes called the
Judgment-seat of David, an exquisite little open
building, consisting practically of a dome and
two sets of pillars to support it, the inner ones
being arranged in a hexagonal shape, while the
outer columns are disposed in eleven sides. It
would be the work of weeks to explore and
chronicle all that is to be seen of this kind, and
we had no such leisure unfortunately. The
building vulgarly called the Tomb of Elias, or

sometimes of St George, with its beautiful carved stone roof, should not be missed. Towards the northern end the most interesting object is the Golden Gate, the double arch of which projects both on the inside and outside of the Haram, though the gate itself has been walled up. There is a tradition, especially strong among Mohammedans, who fear that it may be true, that a Messiah will revisit the earth who will have no respect for the Prophet at all, and drive his followers out of the city to re-establish the Christian rule. He will enter Jerusalem through the Golden Gate, it is said, so the Mussulman authorities have taken the commendable precaution of walling it up to prevent his getting through. Certainly, a Messiah who could not get through a closed-up gate, would not be likely to set even the Jordan on fire. In point of fact, I believe it is only a sort of wicket for foot-passengers which has been closed in even comparatively recent times, as the walling-up of the great gate probably dates from an early period. It is sometimes thought to be "the gate of the outward sanctuary, which looketh toward the east," of which it was said to Ezekiel, "This

gate shall be shut, it shall not be opened,
and no man shall enter in by it; because
the Lord, the God of Israel, hath entered in
by it, therefore it shall be shut." Others
identify it with the Gate Beautiful, where
the lame man was healed by St Peter and
St John,—a tradition founded, I fear, on a
hideous barbarism perpetrated by some unknown translator who rendered the Greek word
ὡραία, "beautiful," into the Latin aurea. There
is a portico inside the closed gate which is
worth visiting, though it is not always easy to
gain admittance.

There is perhaps more to see of interest towards the southern extremity of the Sanctuary.
Leaving the platform of the Rock by the southern stairs, we pass first the pulpit of the Cadi,
from which weekly sermons are delivered during
the month of Ramadan—a marble structure of
exquisite workmanship, supported on arches of
the perfectly circular formation peculiar to Arabian architecture—then an immense stone laver,
shadowed by immemorial cypresses, which might
almost date back to King Solomon's time, and
find ourselves in front of a grand colonnade

forming the entrance to a Christian church. Yes, there is no doubt about it: it is stripped of all its ornaments, and the Mohammedan attributes of *mihrab* and *mimbar* have been introduced into it; but no one can doubt for a moment what it has been. It was here that Justinian, twelve hundred years ago, built a church in honour of our Lady, which was restored to Christian worship by the Templars after some centuries of Mohammedan domination. There is still the great vaulted hall, opening off the church, where the knights of that fiercest of holy brotherhoods met together. Here, in the long bare aisles—not so bare then, we may well imagine—they assembled in prayer, often perhaps as a prelude to some savage raid on the nearest infidel stronghold. Here, however, we are not tempted to remember their faults. We are rather inclined to wish that their days had come back, and that we might see them ride clattering into the court again, breaking down the ensigns of Mohammedan worship with their heavy maces, and restoring the holy city to—well, probably to be fought over by half-a-dozen Christian sects, all at bitter enmity, and " hating one another for the love of God." I fear that we must be content for the present to leave Jerusalem under the direction of the Turkish Pasha, at this moment, no doubt, much troubled in his mind about the dangerous ceremony of the " Holy Fire," which is to take place this very afternoon, and quaking with apprehension at the news that forty stout man-of-warsman have come up for the feast from a Russian ironclad lying off Jaffa. What if it should occur to them—as it actually did—to ask their priests whether they should allow Turkish soldiery on this day of all others to stand round the sepulchre of the risen Lord ? These apprehensions are groundless, however. The good Greek priests, even if they are not always in charity with their neighbours, will do their duty to - day in preaching peace to the exasperated sailors, and the Pasha will once more be able to telegraph to Constantinople that the perilous season has passed over without incident. It is best to be at peace with all men. If we are to take any revenge on the Mussul-man possessors of what we are hardly worthy to hold till we have learned to apply the pre-

cepts of our own religion, let it be something in
the style of the carver of that splendid pulpit,
an evidently Christian artist, who has played
his Mohammedan masters the trick of introduc-
ing in his designs the hated sign of the cross, a
fact which has apparently escaped their notice
to this day.

The hall of the Templars runs from the western side of what must have been the choir of
the Church of Our Lady. In curious contrast
to this relic of the Christian occupation is the
building opening off the eastern side opposite.
It is a small and rather bare chapel—if we may
so use the word—chiefly remarkable for some
curious early Byzantine stone-work, but it has
a distinct historical interest as being in all
probability the real Mosque of the Caliph Omar,
a term often incorrectly applied either to the
whole of the Sanctuary enclosure or to the
Dome of the Rock. The Mohammedan chron-
iclers tell us how the Caliph was brought to the
site of the Temple by the Christian Patriarch,
and how he knelt down to say his prayers
afterwards in the Christian church, which even
then stood on the site of the present Mosque

of El Aksa, and spat upon his tunic to show his detestation of the manner in which it had been polluted by the sin of polytheism. Then he asked his councillor, Ka'ab el Abhar, the renegade Jew, where he should build his mosque, and Ka'ab said in the hinder portion which is toward the north. But Omar said, " No, for the fore part of the Sanctuary belongs to us." Ka'ab el Abhar was probably one of the biggest liars who ever lived ; but El Walid ibn Muslim, who is made responsible for the story by the author of the Muthir, may have been a reliable man. It seems at least very probable that Omar selected this spot for his mosque. The small chapel in question is probably the only building of Omar's which remains to us. The others are of greatly varying dates ; the Dome of the Rock was erected by Abd-el-Melek, some fifty years after the capture of Jerusalem by the Mohammedans.

Somehow we seem to have lost sight of the Temple itself all this while. But of the Temple there is really nothing remaining but the place. We certainly find pillars and stones of great antiquity, remnants of former great works, em-

ployed again in the Mohammedan constructions;
but these can be of little service in giving even
a general idea of the original building. Those
who wish to know more must be content to see
with the eyes of Warren and Wilson, and the
various explorers who have made researches
here and published their discoveries; for the
authorities will only permit excavations on the
condition that all the treasures unearthed are to
be carefully covered up again. The rest of us
must be content with the place alone, the
general scene of many incidents in our Lord's
life, chiefly preserved for us by St John. If
there are no remains of the ancient buildings
to guide us in reconstructing these, it is an
advantage, on the other hand, that there are
no traditional sites pointed out, except those
connected with the Mohammedan fairy-tales,
of which Solomon is usually the hero.

With the Temple and Calvary we have ex-
hausted almost all the scenes at all directly
connected with the Gospel story which are
within the walls of Jerusalem. There is, however, a building to the extreme south of the
city, and actually outside the walls, which con-

tains a chamber identified by tradition with that in which the Last Supper took place. The tradition is said not to be of the greatest antiquity : indeed, we are told that in St Helena's time this spot was revered as the place where the Holy Ghost descended upon the apostles after the Crucifixion. The country just outside the walls is full of memories of Old and New Testament history. There are the steep slopes of the Mount of Olives, where our Lord apparently had His simple resting-place during most of His visits to Jerusalem, whether in the hut of some peasant disciple, or in the open among the olive plantations, as many poor men sleep now, with no roof above Him but the great canopy of heaven, which is His throne. At the foot of the hill, opposite the eastern wall of the Temple enclosure, is one of the most sacred spots, the Garden of Gethsemane : the piety of the early Christians had covered it with shrines and chapels, but it has now fortunately returned to its primitive use as a garden, entertained with loving care by the Franciscans, to whom it belongs. The principal feature of the garden is the group of ancient olive-trees, very

possibly descendants of those which stood here
in the time of the Gospel. A most interesting
walk can be taken from here along the Valley
of Jehoshaphat,—generally known to the indig-
enous Christians as the Valley of the Lady
Mary (Wady Sitti Maryam), because it con-
tains the traditional tomb of the Virgin,—which
skirts the eastern side of the city and the
Temple enclosure. On the eastern slope of the
valley are several curious sepulchral monuments,
all carefully identified by tradition as the tomb
of Absalom—the " pillar in the king's dale,"
which he reared up for himself—of Jehoshaphat
of St James, and of Zachariah. The Christians
take the last named to be the father of St John
the Baptist, while the Jews prefer to identify
him with Zechariah, the son of Jehoiada, who
was stoned in the court of the Temple in the
days of King Joash. The Koran solves all
difficulties by declaring that not only these
two Zechariahs, but also Zechariah, the son
of Barachiah, were in reality one and the
same person. The Prophet was not strong in
chronology. Beyond the tombs comes the
picturesque little village of Siloam, a group

of white flat-roofed houses, perched half-way
up the hill; while, almost opposite, is the
entrance to the subterranean Pool of Siloam.
Further on down the valley, on the road to
Mar Saba, is the historic fountain of En Rogel,
where Adonijah held his famous feast. We
turn to the right, before reaching it, under
the wild hill where tradition places the Field
of Blood, and so up the Valley of Hinnom,
and past the Pools of Gihon to the Jaffa Gate.
Many other small excursions of interest may
be made by those whose time is not limited;
but for most of the places more intimately
connected with the Bible story, one must go
rather farther afield.

IV.

THE NEIGHBOURHOOD OF JERUSALEM : BETHLEHEM,
BETHANY, JERICHO, AND THE DEAD SEA.

IF it could be cast up to Bethlehem in ancient
days that she was little among the thousands of
Judah, there could at least have been few of the
rival cities that had a prettier or pleasanter site.
There is something peculiarly attractive in the
first view of the little white town, nestling into
a nook of the hills, with the great basilica of the
Nativity standing out at one end, the mother-
building of the city, in a proud supremacy
unchallenged by mosque or synagogue; for the
people of Bethlehem, with few exceptions, are
Christians. The scene is full of memories, too;
the fields in the valley below us are those where
Ruth gleaned after the reapers, and David watched

his father's sheep. There, too, those other shep-
herds watched many centuries later who saw the
heavenly host singing glory to God in the highest ;
and over the road we have just travelled came
those mysterious sages from the far East, whose
learning had somehow opened to them the
knowledge concealed from all other men but the
handful of rough peasants who knelt with them
by the side of the cradle. The town indeed is
of little interest, but there is a cheery kindly
air about the people who crowd round the
carriage with smiles of welcome—and perhaps,
also, of anticipated profit, for few visitors leave
Bethlehem without expending ruinous sums on
the wonderful mother-of-pearl work for which
the place is famous. But of this we cannot yet
think, before our pilgrimage is accomplished.

We had some apprehensions, as we entered
the stately Greek church, that here, too, we
should find an excessive wealth of ecclesiastical
ornament concealing from us what we wished to
see ; but it was not of this that we had to complain. The Grotto of the Nativity is at least
recognisable in form for what it may have been
when the Holy Family were sheltered here, and

the ornamentation is in good taste. The traditional site of the Nativity is marked by a single
silver star, above which hang the lamps placed
there in pious emulation by the various Christian
sects. Happy would it be if their rivalry could
stop there, so that the devout pilgrim might be
spared the sore sight of the Turkish sentinel
posted over against that sacred spot. It is
impossible to imagine a keener satire on Christian
doctrine and Christian practice than is afforded
by the spectacle of an infidel soldier standing on
guard before the cradle of the Prince of Peace,
to prevent his disciples from flying at each
other's throats. The sentry is stationed here
by the Turkish authorities—with two or three
comrades within call, sitting on the steps leading
to the choir of the Greek church above—not
as an insult to Christian sentiment, as one is
tempted to imagine at first, but as a *bonâ fide*
precaution, the necessity of which has been
shown. It is not so very long since, we were
told, the Greek and Latin priests came actually
to blows in the church ; and the dormant ill-feel-
ing which always remains between the sects, is
unfortunately excited afresh by any occasion of

special religious enthusiasm.[1] One wonders rather that this fanatic spirit is never directed against the Mohammedans, the natural object of enmity to both parties alike. The idea does seem to occur to them occasionally. As I stood in the grotto there came in a very wild-looking Arab convert, under the conduct of a venerable Franciscan with an immense grey beard, who, while kneeling and kissing the sacred spots with great veneration, varied his devotions by casting furious glances at the unconscious sentinel. It would have made a good picture, — the old Franciscan in the plain brown gown of his Order pointing to one spot after the other, and mingling, apparently, his explanations with seasonable moral lessons ; the tall, sinewy, handsome Arab, in his black-and-white striped burnouse, listening with all his ears, but glancing back with a kind of tigerish glare in his eyes at the third and least attractive figure of the scene, the coarse shabby Turkish soldier, with his dirty blue uniform and his heavy sensual face.

[1] Since this was written another and even more serious riot has taken place between the Greek and Latin Christians at Bethlehem.

From the Grotto of the Nativity, a narrow passage cut in the solid rock leads to other traditional sites, of which the most probably genuine is the cell of St Jerome, a saint very dear and familiar to us in Italian painting, with his attendant lion and his piles of books, strangely numerous for an anchorite's retreat—perhaps less popular with the students of his life. It was here, perhaps, that he did his greatest work, the translation of the Scriptures into a language understanded of the people, a work the use of which has so oddly survived him into ages when the people do not understand it in the least; here, certainly, that he spirited away poor Paula and her daughter to live out their lives in futile austerity, thousands of miles from home and kindred. The admixture of these kind of associations with the more sacred traditions made us, perhaps, less unwilling to return to the upper air, which we reached at last, after many windings through the corridors cut in the rock, in the Latin church of St Catherine. This is also a sufficiently stately edifice, though somewhat over-decorated, but not to be compared with the magnificent basilica in which the Greek

E

services are celebrated. The Greeks seem to have rather the best of it here, as indeed is generally the case in the Holy Land. The Latins have, indeed, their chapel opening out of the Grotto of the Nativity, but the access to it can only be through these dark subterranean passages, unless by sufferance of their Greek brethren. So it is that on great festival days the Latin processions have to pass to their chapel across the Greek church, through a passage guarded by a double line of Turkish soldiers with loaded rifles. There is here, perhaps, an excess of precaution, emphasised by official distrust of Christianity, Greek or Latin; though the love that the opposing Churches bear to each other is certainly more after the manner of St Jerome than in imitation of the Founder of the common faith.

As Bethlehem shows us the beginning of the Gospel story, Bethany is chiefly connected with its end. Bethany—or El Azariyeh as the Mohammedans call it, after Lazarus, who holds a high rank in their hagiology—is now a poor village, presenting a ruinous, but not particularly picturesque, appearance from the highroad. It

is crammed with traditional sites—the house
of Mary and Martha, the house of Simon the
Pharisee, the tomb of Lazarus—all of equally
doubtful authenticity. A higher interest is
given to the locality from the fact that the
ascension of our Lord must have taken place on
some point near here, though authorities differ
greatly as to the exact spot. I remember standing on the gallery of the minaret of the dervishes'
monastery on the top of the Mount of Olives,
and looking down on a long train of Coptic
women crowding into the little chapel which
covers the traditional place, while our dragoman
pointed out to us a round green hill covered
with stones in the neighbourhood of Bethany as
the situation selected by the latest explorers. It
is all more or less guess-work, of course, though
St Luke's account is clear enough as to the distance from Jerusalem, and the traditional place
on the Mount of Olives can hardly be received
as possible. The whole neighbourhood here
forms a part of the country most trodden by our
Lord during His visits to Jerusalem. And there
is one among the traditional sites which is un-
utterably touching, for which not tradition only,

but the words of the Gospel and the evidence of
the situation vouch,—that corner of the road at
the turn of the hill where our Lord, on His last
journey into Jerusalem, first caught sight of the
city, and, in the midst of the praise and rejoic-
ings which accompanied His last progress, burst
forth into that saddest outbreak of divine regret
and compassion, "If thou hadst known!" Terribly solemn words, even to read; a lament to
be echoed for ages by those whose eyes are
opened in a new world to their fearful mistaking.
For ourselves, strengthened by preceding centuries of belief, we are inclined, with a consciousness of our feeble insight into what is
really good or bad, to thank God that we were
not born in the days when the faith of man was
tested by so awful a trial.

Our way to Jericho took us past most of
these spots, and between the villages of Bethany
and Bethphage, an interesting commencement to
a toilsome and monotonous journey. The greater
part of it lay through a succession of barren,
sun-beaten wadies, the very sight of which
gives one an anticipatory sense of weariness.
The only relief to the monotony was afforded

by meeting with our old friends the Russian pilgrims, trudging sturdily back from a pilgrimage to the Jordan, with bundles of reeds gathered on its banks in their hands. Merely to see them fling themselves down in utter weariness by the Apostles' Fountain, was sufficient to tell one what a real pilgrimage is, with real hardships quietly borne as necessary incidents in such a journey, and a real purpose to carry them through it all. It is a pleasure to meet these honest simple Russians, with their plain genuine devotion. In a few days we would see them starting off for Jaffa, with their faces turned homewards at last, and that journey they have looked forward to with so many hopes and doubts at least half over: one or two of the luckiest had managed to hire donkeys, but the rest trudged along with an air of perfect contentment and pride in the treasures they were bringing home,—the reeds from the Jordan, the tapers that had been lit with the holy fire, and the long tin cylinders containing the sacred pictures that had been laid upon the Holy Sepulchre. As we met them now, the quiet patience of their faces rather shamed us from grumbling at the road, which is in course of making, and has been so for a considerable time. At the present rate of progression, we calculated that it should be finished towards the close of the twenty-second century, and even then it is doubtful whether it would be safe for a carriage.

The chief break in this toilsome journey, besides the picturesque Apostles' Fountain, is afforded by the half-way khan, sometimes called The Khan of the Good Samaritan. It was our first experience of such a place of entertainment, and we were somewhat curious as to what we should find there. It consists of a large square enclosure, most of which is uncovered; on the side facing the road, however, are a small building on one side of the gate, where the keeper of the khan lives, and opposite it a cool pleasant colonnade, where the weary traveller can enjoy such provisions as he has brought with him in comparative comfort. The guardian of the establishment can supply coffee or lemonade, but these appear to form the limit of his resources. However, a khan is seldom a place of public entertainment in our sense: the shelter

from heat or bad weather is usually all that it
professes to provide, something on the same
principle as an Alpine hut in Switzerland. And
certainly, the one thing for which the traveller
to Jericho longs is shade, and he is not likely
to be very hard to please when this is provided
for him. On a hill above the khan are the
very dilapidated ruins of an ancient crusading
fort. Further along the road the curious inquirer
may learn the exact spot where the man in the
parable fell among thieves. There is, of course,
no reason to suppose that any such person ever
existed; but it is interesting to note that the
road which our Lord chose as the scene of
His apologue has been always infested by
brigands up to a very recent date.

The long-wished-for goal was reached at last;
we came finally to a height where there are no
further obstacles between us and the view of
the valley of the Jordan, and after struggling
down a long and steep descent we emerged from
the wilderness into a pleasant land of grass and
water. We had found some relief already from
the heat and aridity of the surroundings in
the cool murmur of the brook Cherith, many

hundred feet below the road we were travelling on; but the sudden plunge into this valley was none the less delightful. A beautiful and rich country truly, and better watered than perhaps any spot I have seen in Palestine, but not a prosperous one; the fields are scantily cultivated, and great tracts of good land are turned to no use whatever. Nor can we blame the natives for the lack of enterprise which fails to utilise the great resources of their country. With a jealous exacting Government on the one side, and lawless tribes of predatory Bedouins on the other, the native cultivator finds himself in a manner between the devil and the deep sea, and we can hardly require him to expend capital and labour, if neither he nor his can count upon reaping the fruits. But it is a sad sight to see all this rich land going to waste.

Of Jericho itself there is very little to be seen. It is a place whose annals have been very full and troubled, and has undergone many ups and downs of glory and degradation since it was first laid low by Joshua. There is but a handful of rude huts now to mark the place of it, and the only vestiges of its former grandeur are the great stones that once formed part of some palace or temple now built into the wall of a miserable Arab hovel. There is much that is interesting in the neighbourhood for those who have time and strength and health to endure a stay in that furnace of a valley. Few Europeans can stand the climate; to those who have to spend much time in Palestine there is no bugbear like Jericho fever. But for a day or two it may be very pleasant, though the heat is pretty sure to be tremendous.

The usual plan for tourists is to make a three days' excursion from Jerusalem, spending one whole day at Jericho, when an excursion can be made to the Dead Sea and the Jordan. Our way to the sea leads us quickly out of the fertile land which surrounds Jericho itself, over a bare sandy plain, the aspect of which becomes more and more desolate as we go on. On our right rise the bleak mountains of the wilderness of Judah, which we traversed on our way here: one of the most rugged and barren among them, honeycombed with the caves of anchorites of old, in the midst of which now stands a little

Abyssinian monastery, is pointed out as the traditional site of our Lord's fast of forty days. Further to the north, a high peaked hill is regarded as the place from which Satan showed all the kingdoms of the world; this tradition, however, is a little weakened by the discovery that the top of the hill, far from dominating the kingdoms around, is actually below the level of the Mediterranean. This may serve to show us how far down we must be in the valley.

The country through which we approached the Dead Sea was dismal and desolate enough to satisfy the gloomiest anticipations, but the sea itself came as an agreeable surprise to us. We had already seen it in the distance from the minaret on the Mount of Olives,—a mere dark-blue line, which formed a picturesque enough contrast to the dark mountains of Moab behind; but we had imagined that only the enchant-ment of distance could give it any beauty. As a point of fact, it is, as seen from the northern shore, an extremely pretty lake of a beautiful deep blue, flanked by mountains of sufficiently picturesque outline and a peculiar richness of colouring, which includes every varying shade

of red and brown; of green there is none in
this desert country. The foreground is spoilt
by a dirty disreputable little island of stones
and *débris* of all kinds, which lies close to
the northern shore : if one could get across
to this, the view would probably be a more
perfect one ; but I cannot recommend any
traveller to a course which would bring him
into personal contact with the slimy sticky
water, the touch and taste of which goes far
to justify all the abuse which has been heaped
upon the Dead Sea.

From here a pleasant canter across the plain,
which becomes green and full of foliage as we
approach the Jordan, brought us to the bank of
the river, at the spot where tradition is pleased
to see the place of our Lord's baptism, and
also of the passage of Joshua and the Israelites from Moab. The former event is now believed to have taken place much higher up the
stream, at a place which is still called Abarah,
the Bethabara beyond Jordan of St John. The
first sight of the Jordan was most disappointing,
the stream, which was swollen by recent rains,
being of a turbid yellow colour, which com-

pared most disadvantageously with the deep
blue of the Dead Sea. The banks, however,
are fairly well wooded—though we grumbled
much at the illusion of shade offered by the
scanty foliage of the tamarisk-trees—and if
the water were only of a better colour, and
the stream a trifle broader, there are some nice
glimpses of river scenery, especially at those
sharp bends and curves to which the Jordan
seems to be partial. We were rather inclined,
however, to adopt Naaman's disparaging view
of the little river; only we found afterwards
that Abana and Pharpar, though as pretty
rivulets as one would wish to see, were not a
bit larger.

The return to Jericho is made over broad
green plains, which make delightful galloping-
ground and produce some singular displays of
horsemanship among pilgrims unaccustomed to
equestrian exercise. The evening at Jericho
was enlivened by a Bedouin dance in front of
a great fire built in the open outside the little
hotel, a long-drawn-out business of posturing,
advancing, and retreating, varied by the eccen-
tric movements of an Indian dervish, who

vapoured about with a drawn sword in the middle of all the wild figures, and from time to time affected to throw himself into the fire, though apparently taking care, like Mr Mantalini, to keep a good twelve inches away from it. Chilling doubts were thrown upon the genuineness of the "Bedouin" dance; "it was a trite affair," as Anthony à Wood said of the herald's visitation, "and many thought it a trick to get money." Next morning we were all glad to turn our faces towards Jerusalem again, and greeted the sight of the Holy City this time with a genuine joy at the end of the long wearisome road. An early start should be made on the return journey, which is fatiguing at the best, and is rendered much more toilsome by the intense heat in the middle of the day.

V.

MOUNT CARMEL.

IT was with a somewhat uncomfortable feeling that we made our first plunge into the unknown in the classic region of Carmel. So far, we had been travelling along well-trodden ways by known methods of conveyance, and sleeping under more or less solid roofs ; but here, at Haifa, we were to commence a life of wandering and dwelling in tents, with little prospect of finding civilisation nearer than Damascus. To emphasise our separation from the rest of mankind, we must begin by being in a manner marooned at Haifa—being dropped from our good European steamer, full of commonplace tourists *en route* for Beyrout, at the dead of night into a clumsy native boat, manned by decidedly unskilful oarsmen—and felt a certain

pride at the sight of the retinue which was waiting on the pier with paper lanterns to light us
on our way to the camp. It is upon record that
Mr Boswell, when he was summoned to dinner
at Fort George by tuck of drum, felt a moment-
ary pride in imagining himself to be a soldier :
we were tempted to flatter ourselves that there
must really be something adventurous about our
enterprise, with all these unusual surroundings.
It was a pleasant illusion which we conscien-
tiously endeavoured to keep up, even when the
surroundings had become terribly matter-of-fact,
and we found our table constantly supplied with
the veriest Cockney delicacies.

The waking in strange lands was here an
auspicious one. The morning was fine, and the
bay of Haifa lay before us, an unbroken sheet of
tranquil blue, set off by the reddish colour of
the sands beyond. The historic city of Acre
was just visible through the morning haze on the
further shore, and over the low hills behind it
we could catch at rare intervals a glimpse of the
snow-capped summit of that shiest of mountains,
Hermon,—with which we were destined in time
to become much better acquainted. Behind us

rose the northern slopes of Mount Carmel—not
very interesting in appearance from this side
—on which, just above the promontory which
closed our view to the westward, stood out the
great monastery, a disappointing building, with
none of the venerable attributes which should
distinguish the mother of all the Carmelite
establishments in the world. It is, in point of
fact, not seventy years old; and even its prede-
cessor, which was destroyed by the Turks some
years before the present building was erected,
only dated from the seventeenth century. The
Order, of course, is of much greater antiquity;
but its fortunes have fluctuated, and many suc-
cessive monasteries have been built and destroyed since its first institution. All that I
can say of the present building is that it gives to
the otherwise bare hillside that sign of the presence of something living which always adds interest to a landscape; and, as the guide-books
say, the traveller who visits it will be rewarded
with a fine view : there is no gainsaying that.

There is, of course, in this neighbourhood no
connection with any part of the history which
gives the greatest interest to the Holy Land;

and even in the Old Testament there is little
of interest in connection with Mount Carmel,
except the one great scene of Elijah's contest
with the prophets of Baal. But it appears,
nevertheless, from the earliest times to have
been endued with a peculiar sanctity, of which
it has lost nothing to this day in the eyes of
Christian, Jew, or Moslem. Perhaps this may
account for the remarkable gathering of all
varieties of sects which is found in the neighbourhood of the Carmel range. The Mohammedans, who are considerably outnumbered by the
Christians and Jews, are not so well represented;
yet there is at Acre a Persian prophet of great
eminence, who has announced himself to be the
Bab, or Gate of Salvation, through whom the
Deity must be approached, and is regarded with
the profoundest reverence by the Mussulmans,
especially those of his own country. Indeed, a
story is told of a Persian nobleman who offered
to give up all his possessions to this prophet on
condition of being allowed to serve him even in
the humblest capacity,—an advantageous offer
which the holy man accepted. In the town of
Haifa itself, the Melchites predominate—a curi-

F

ous sect who appear to hover upon the frontiers of the Greek and Roman beliefs without distinctly belonging to either. The Latins, indeed, have the benefit of their avowed adherence; but their practices must be much more satisfactory to the Greeks. They are, in fact, proselytes from the Greek Church, who stipulated as the price of their conversion that they should be allowed to retain their former customs upon three unimportant points,—the marriage of the clergy, the administration of the communion in both kinds to the congregation, and the celebration of the service in the vernacular. These trifling concessions having been granted, they accepted the supremacy of the Pope and the Latin date of Easter without further difficulty.

Moslem or Christian, Greek or Latin, have done little in all the years they have had for the improvement, material and moral, of the town or neighbourhood. But in the last twenty years the Christian population has been increased by the arrival of a new contingent of a very different character. In our camp we were some distance from the narrow crooked streets of the Arab town, but a few steps brought us into a broad level road, bordered by double lines of trees and substantial well-built houses, the very model of the *chaussée* of some little German summer resort. We were in the colony of the German Society of the Temple, which perhaps we may consider the most extraordinary of all the sects assembled here. It is the rule of this singular people not to enter deeply into matters of doctrine—or, at any rate, to leave a great latitude for individual opinion—but simply to carry out in their lives the principles laid down in the Gospels,—a strange idea, indeed, but rather a sensible one when one comes to think of it. They have, indeed, some beliefs of their own, as that the second advent is at hand, and that it will take place in Palestine, so that they have come here to be on the spot. There are other colonies at Jaffa and Jerusalem, as well as in Germany, America, and Russia: I believe Haifa was selected for the first settlement merely from reasons of convenience. The greater number of the colonists are from Würtemberg, the country of their founder, Professor Christopher Hoffmann, and the adjacent parts of South

Germany and German Switzerland, though a considerable proportion—including Herr Schumacher, the *Vorsteher* of the Haifa community— are German Americans. Of their views we had no means of judging ; their acts speak for themselves. It is to them that all the progress that has been made in this part of the country is due—the peaceful and successful cultivation of the land and the new immunity from brigandage, as also the fact that we could drive through the town from the pier in what could by courtesy be termed a carriage, over something remotely resembling a road—and, generally, all the recent improvements. The peasantry are said to be greatly impressed with this new kind of Christians, whose honesty and benevolence can really be relied on ; the traveller will be equally struck with their invariable friendliness and hospitality to strangers.

Our own pilgrimage to Mount Carmel was chiefly to see the scenes in which Laurence Oliphant spent the last years of his life. The man who can claim any connection of kindred or friendship with him is very welcome on Mount Carmel. The Germans have a loving recollection of him, and the Druses in the villages of the hills entertain an almost superstitious veneration for his memory and that of Sitti Alice, his wife. Few, indeed, of the inhabitants whom we meet but have stories to tell of his practical love of his neighbour, and his chivalrous devotion to the cause of all whom he found to be oppressed. The case of the Roumanian Jews, who were sent out here by the Jewish Colonising Society of their country, and who, finding no preparations made to receive them, were left upon the streets of Haifa, homeless, penniless, and starving, till Laurence Oliphant took them up, maintaining the whole number at his own expense till satisfactory arrangements could be made for the establishment of the colony, is one of the best known cases. But his chief work lay among the Druses, with whom he lived for half the year at the little village of Daliyeh, high up on Mount Carmel. Our road to Galilee was to pass over the hills by Daliyeh, a recognised station of our pilgrimage, and for this we accordingly started from Haifa under the guidance of Laurence's friend and successor, Mr Haskett Smith.

The first part of our journey was performed in a rough kind of conveyance, a sort of covered *char-à-bancs*, driven by an honest German who proudly asserted that he had driven the Herr and Frau Oliphant fifty times at least. The road lay across the long level plain which stretches along the coast from Carmel as far as Jaffa. It was smooth and good till after we had passed the pretty Friedhof, where the mortal remains of Alice Oliphant are laid, but after that degenerated into a rough track, with cultivated fields on one side of it, and on the other the singular natural barrier of rock which shuts off the sea-coast from the plain for many miles. A couple of hours' drive brought us to the ruins of the great crusading fortress of Athlit, which we approached through a passage cut out of the rock barrier. Here, in a pleasant green meadow near a little pond fringed with English-looking willows, our luncheon-tent was pitched, and here, too, the son of the Druse sheikh was waiting for us with a small following,—a fine, martial-looking fellow, whose appearance was somewhat impaired by an old European greatcoat, which he persisted in wearing over his picturesque national dress, and of which, ugly and inappropriate as it was, he was inordinately proud. The ruins of Athlit lie out of the way of most travellers, and are not so often visited as they should be. It is difficult to imagine anything more impressive than the great grim ruin rising out of the sea on this exposed point, the waves dashing up within a few feet of the mouldering pillars of the ruined banqueting-hall, and the dirty miserable Arab village forcing its way into all available nooks and crannies, like some foul parasite feeding on the decay of the noble building. The outer wall of the north tower is still standing, an imposing pile, in spite of wind and weather and vandal Turks, who regard ruins generally as quarries for building materials; but the most striking of all is the great hall by the sea, where the Templars met together for the last time before leaving Palestine, when every other stronghold had been taken by the Saracens, and the ships were waiting in the little bay outside to carry away even this last remnant of the Christian garrisons.

The rest of the way lay up Mount Carmel itself, along a winding path, skirting the picturesque Arab village of Ainhout and ascending through a pleasant country abounding in flowers and small trees, till we came in sight of the long low white house built by Laurence Oliphant for a summer residence, and still inhabited by a little group of his friends. The Druse village lies close by. Every traveller has written something of this strange nation of the Druses, but few have been able to get any certain information. Neither the family of nations to which they belong nor the country from which they come can be decided with anything like certainty. The purity of the Arabic spoken by them has made some suppose them to be emigrants from the south of Arabia, while others regard them as an Aryan race from eastern Asia, a theory borne out by their fair complexions, blue eyes, and generally un-Semitic appearance. Others, again, see in them the survivors of a very ancient population inhabiting the same districts in which they are found to-day, from Aleppo to Mount Carmel. Their religion, again, is a thing entirely apart from either Christian, Jewish, or Moslem beliefs, though some traditions of the other faiths appear to have crept into it. It is

ostensibly taken with their name from one
Duruzi, a Mohammedan heretic of the eleventh
century, who, however, appears rather to have
aimed at founding a political party than a
religious sect; perhaps his teaching was merely
embroidered on to an older religion. For reasons
best known to himself, Duruzi supported the
assertion of the then Caliph, the mad Hakim
Biamrillah, that he was an incarnation of Allah,
and the Druses are still waiting for that person-
age's reappearance upon earth — which should
happen in some thirty years' time—when the
world will come to an end. The holiest mysteries of their beliefs are not even known to all
Druses, but only to the initiated among them :
it is possible, however, that, as with other great
mysteries, there is not very much to reveal.
One of their most singular ideas is that there
are many Druses in England and also in China
—the latter being unaware of the fact themselves
—with which country they would appear to have
some mysterious connection.   That they should
even be aware of its existence is sufficiently as-
tonishing.

The Druses have been a great nation in their

day; indeed, the few Druse communities scattered about Galilee are the descendants of the conquerors of a former day, who subdued the whole country from Aleppo to Carmel, under their great leader Fakr-ed-Din. But their days of prosperity are past; they are still sufficiently formidable in the Hauran—a district south-east of Damascus, sometimes known as the Druse Mountain — and in the Lebanon, where they share the advantages of that privileged province with their deadly enemies, the Maronites. But the Druse of Galilee is a sojourner in a strange land, disliked by both Christians and Mohammedans, and plundered by the Government which he is not strong enough to resist. When Laurence Oliphant came to Mount Carmel, he found the unhappy Druses in despair, overburdened with apparently hopeless arrears of taxes, and he set himself to work to retrieve their position, so far with considerable success. Certainly, the community at present has a very decent appearance of prosperity.

They are a kindly people, and gave us almost as cordial a welcome as our kind friends in Laurence Oliphant's house, to whose good offices we owed most of our favour with the Druses, and on whom we were obliged to depend entirely for any manner of communication with the latter, from our lamentable ignorance of the language. Under their guidance we were generally made free of the village, and solemnly received by the principal sheikh, a genial-looking old man with a bronzed weather-beaten face, and very white hair and beard. We were taken across a courtyard into a large, bare, vaulted room, with queer openings like windows, through which occasionally heads of men, or other animals, were pushed in to see what was going on. The bulk of the population followed us in, men, women, and children, — the Druse women are mostly pretty, by the way,—flocking in and stacking themselves somehow in corners as Eastern people know the trick of doing, till the room simply swarmed with human beings. Some of the most important had already been presented to us, including a very fine-looking old priest, and the village doctor, a venerable old humbug, who, I could not help thinking, would be safe of a baronetcy in England for his looks alone. I might have suggested his coming

over for the purpose, as the Druses are very
friendly to England—who stood by them when
they were in danger of being wiped off the face
of the earth in return for the crimes of a few
among them, after the Damascus massacres in
1860—but, alas! there was that sad ignorance
of the Arabic tongue, which limited my powers
of conversation to such weighty remarks as
"good morning" and "thank you." It was an
opportunity lost for both of us.

We were to have seen an exhibition of native
dancing, and were regaled for some time with
cinnamon-tea while the preliminaries were arranged. But we never were allowed to see more
than a dance of men, which was not very interesting, though one of the dancers, a Druse from
the Hauran, who had just come to Daliyeh to
see his relations, was held to be a master of
the art. Nothing would persuade the women to
dance unless the men were quite out of reach—
though nothing can be more decorous than the
Druse women's dance. One little blue-eyed
girl was half persuaded, half bullied into beginning some steps at last; but she had hardly
commenced before shyness got the better of her,

and she covered her face with her hands, and darted back into the shelter of the crowd.

By the time we had seen so much, or so little, the sun was already high in the heavens, and as we had to get as far as Nazareth that day, it was necessary to make a start. We had arranged to go up to the little Latin *hospice*, built in commemoration of Elijah's contest with the prophets of Baal on one of the peaks of Carmel, and descend from there to the plain of Esdraelon, over which our way to Nazareth would lie. Our road took us through a smiling country of verdure and flowers—Carmel is celebrated for its flowers. Masses of asphodel, cistus of every kind, cyclamen, anemones, all kinds of flowers, clothed the earth as with a carpet,—

"Of Nature's couch the living tapestry,"

as good Bishop Gavin hath it,—while, finest of all were the great gorgeous hollyhocks, that light up the further slopes with their brilliant colouring. The little chapel of the Carmelites at the place called Elijah's altar is of no great interest, though it commands a fine view; but it is easy to see that it cannot be the actual place of his sacrifice, nor does it probably pretend to be so. Once the neighbourhood of the scene to be commemorated had been reached, the chapel would be built simply on the most convenient spot. The probable real scene of the famous contest was shown to us a little farther on, when we had begun the descent. Here there is a great green amphitheatre, where a vast multitude of people might be assembled. On one side is a fountain which is believed never to run dry,—the reader will remember that in spite of the great drought there appears to have been no difficulty in finding the water which Elijah asked for. The steep slope, down which we had to make our way to the plain, might very well have been the scene of the desperate flight of the priests of Baal, pursued by the mob of Israelites in all the ardour of a very new conversion, burning to expiate their backslidings by the slaughter of somebody else, and the river Kishon would naturally be the first barrier to their escape. The sea is not in sight from the place mentioned, — indeed we had turned our backs upon it ; but Elijah's servant could easily have run up to the top of the ridge, from which he could see over the Mediterranean far away to the westward. I have rarely, even in the Holy Land, been brought so perfectly face to face with a scene from any history, as in that dell of Carmel.

From the heights we thus traversed a really magnificent view was obtained, both of what we were leaving behind us and of the country we had yet to travel through. Coming suddenly upon the landscape, as we did at the summit of the ridge, there was something very striking in the aspect of the great plain of Esdraelon below us. There is an air of peace and prosperity about the broad level expanse, checkered with the various colours of the different crops, with the little river Kishon winding its way through the midst of it. Yet it has been known as a battle-field for more than three thousand years, and all its memories are of blood. It was from that queer round hill of Tabor over against us, that Barak and his host dashed down upon the army of Sisera as they laboured through the partly inundated plain, which made their dreaded chariots a mere encumbrance : here, many centuries later, was the scene of one of the last combats of Christian and Moslem; and here, too, after a lapse of five hundred years more, the Mohammedans had to encounter a very different enemy in the rough French heroes, who questioned each other on the march (as one of their number relates),—" Qu'est-ce-que c'est que la Terre Sainte? Pourquoi ce nom-là?" The country where the new Gospel of peace and love has left its traditions lies among the hills beyond. The glimpse of white on the two-peaked hill to the east of Mount Tabor is the end of the village of Nain; and another white building to the west we were told was above Nazareth, which was to be our halting-place for that night. It seemed discouragingly far away from us.

VI.

GALILEE.

THE road across the plain of Esdraelon was not an interesting one, except for the as yet novel incident of fording the Kishon; but when we got among the small hills about Nazareth, the scenery became less monotonous. We were rather late on the road, having started late, and were constantly coming upon groups of picturesquely attired country people returning from their work in the fields to one of the many villages we passed on the way. Nazareth itself was reached just before nightfall. Turning the corner of one of the hills, we came suddenly upon it, a rather ghostly-looking mass of white buildings staring out in the waning light from their background of dark trees. Lights were beginning to flash out at

G

various points along the hillside, and at one
place a broad glare marked the scene of a
wedding-feast, which was carried on to a late
hour with much shouting and discharging of
guns — the usual sign of rejoicing in these
parts.   It was quite dark by the time we
arrived at our camp, and there was nothing
to be seen for that night but the stores of a
few merchants of native metal ornaments, who
made their way to our tents ; while our dragoman, who was a Nazarene by birth, gave audience to flocks of cousins outside.   In the morning
we made the little round of visits to the various
spots connected with the sacred story.   They
are not very striking.   The sanctity of the
house of the Virgin and the scene of the
Annunciation, in the crypt of the Latin church,
was somewhat spoiled for us by the appendage
of the Loretto legend ; but the kind of cave-
dwellings shown to us might possibly have
been what they pretend to be.   In another
Latin church we were shown a great block of
stone supposed to have served as a table for
our Lord and His disciples, which is perhaps
also within the bounds of possibility.   I am

not learned enough to say more than that I was by no means inclined to believe it. The so-called "carpenter's shop," where a late tradition says that our Lord and St Joseph worked, we did not feel equal to visiting. There was a kind of atmosphere of *banal* relic-worship about all these sights that only a very strong faith could stand. It is more interesting to know that on the rocky eminence above the quaint little Maronite church probably stood the synagogue of the Gospel days, and the place from which the exasperated Jews would have thrown our Lord down. I have always had a fancy that that famous scene must have been the occasion on which St Luke first saw Him. The story is evidently told by an eyewitness, and the details are so minutely described, that they must have been very deeply impressed upon the mind of the evangelist. Another place of real interest is the Virgin's Fountain, a spring of great antiquity, to which the women of Nazareth still come to fill their pitchers. They make a very pretty group there, with their bright-coloured dresses, but hardly a peaceful one, for bickerings are constantly going on between the

Christian and Moslem women—as, indeed, seems generally to be the case where the former are preponderant. When the Mohammedans are in the majority, their contempt for the Christians produces a certain tolerance.

The next day's journey, to Tiberias, lay in great part over a flat cultivated plain, with few incidents beyond the village of Kefr-Kenna— which may perhaps be Cana of Galilee—and the meeting of some wonderful long strings of camels, bringing probably the grain and other produce of the Hauran down to the sea at Haifa. It grieved us to think how the vested interests of the poor camels and camel-owners might soon be affected when the railway from Haifa to Damascus through the Hauran came to be constructed. However, as the negotiations with the Government about the railway have only been going on now for some seven years, there is little to fear for the present century at least. In the afternoon it was proposed to vary the route by ascending the curious two-peaked hill called the Horns of Hattin, where the Sermon on the Mount is believed to have been delivered. It is a pleasant-looking green hill,

but really very stony, the stones being concealed
by the long rank grass which grows all over
it, and thus made more dangerous. The summit
is covered with grass too, and a few wild flowers,
but only of the commonest kinds—nothing to
compare with the hollyhocks of Carmel, or the
cyclamen of the plain of Sharon. The depression between the two peaks is very slight, and
they are themselves flat-topped; so that it is
conceivable that a considerable crowd might
have accompanied our Lord to the very top—
it is not very high—and sat round Him to hear
the discourse. Or a greater number could have
found place rather lower down, and have been
addressed from the rock at the corner of the
southern and higher platform. From the only
piece of internal evidence, I should incline to
the former theory, which would make the
Preacher face towards the city of Safed, the
extraordinarily prominent position of which, on
a higher hill to the north, is supposed to have
suggested to Him the illustration, " A city that
is set on an hill cannot be hid." The view from
the summit was most beautiful. At our feet lay
the Lake of Tiberias, like a sheet of dark-blue

glass, without a ripple to stir its surface, backed by bare desolate hills, with no sign of life of any kind upon them. In the foreground we had a lower hill, or rather plateau, terminating in a grand ravine, the Wady Hammam, or Valley of Pigeons, the gates of which are two towering masses of rock seeming almost to meet at the top. At the northern end of the lake we caught a glimpse of a low white house, which we afterwards found to be the first step towards a new German colony. Further north, a deep gorge runs up towards Safed, and the holy city itself shines out on the dark hillside with an extraordinary lustre; and still further to the north-west the view is closed in by the wild desert mountains of Naphtali.

The descent upon Tiberias is as beautiful as everything must be that is connected with that lovely lake. Our camp was pitched on its shores some hundreds of yards south of Tiberias itself. Of this little town, the only collection of houses which we ever saw on the lake,—though I believe there is a village at Medjdel, the ancient Magdala,—I can say little, for I was hardly within its walls; but, especially as seen from

the water, it appeared to be one of the most
beautiful places we had yet come across. Per-
haps it was the illusion of the lake which made
us think so, for some camping neighbours who
explored the interior did not seem to be extraordinarily delighted. It is very dirty, and is
inhabited chiefly by Jews; indeed it is, like
Safed, one of their holy cities. Other sects
generally speak of it as the residence of the
king of the fleas, who should certainly be a
great potentate in Palestine. We did not seek
audience of his majesty, having already made
acquaintance with too many of his subjects, but
leaving Tiberias, took boat for the upper end of
the lake. There is a kind of glamour about all
the surroundings here. I had so far kept up a
stolid belief in appearances, and had no doubts
that I really saw Jerusalem or Bethlehem, or
whatever the spot might be; but it seemed
much harder to realise the fact that we were
actually rowing across the Sea of Galilee, and it
required all the discomfort of a cramped position
in a not very roomy boat to prove to us that we
were not dreaming. Our rowers were doing their
utmost, for the dreaded west wind was said to

be coming, and against it we could make little way. But for the time nothing could be more delightful than the tranquil progress over the calm solitary sea. Far away, towards the part where the Jordan flows into the lake, we could catch sight of one white sail—probably a fishing-boat; but there was no sign of any living crea-ture on sea or land as we made for the northern shore by the ruins of Tell Houm. It is strange to think that in the days of the history which gives life and interest to all these scenes, this northern coast was a centre of bustling life and commerce, with the four cities of Capernaum, Bethsaida, Chorazin, and that other one whose ruins are to be found at Tell Houm or Khan Minyeh—whichever is not the site of Caper-naum—looking down upon waters covered with fishing and pleasure boats.

I have never yet seen anything so awful as the desolation of Tell Houm. Here, whether it was Capernaum or not, stood a great city, with evidently a magnificent synagogue. There are yet lying on the ground, half-distinguishable amidst the long grass, broken columns, and great capitals and pediments, and carved stone-work, as they have lain for ages undisturbed, unless by the careless footstep of some passing Arab. A rude hut has been erected near the shore, partly with great stones from the ruins, to form a temporary shelter for some wandering herdsman or his flock; but except for this, for miles around there is not so much as a fisherman's cottage or a peasant's barn,—only the prostrate bones of the dead city mouldering away in the midst of that hideous solitude.

The west wind had come by the time we returned to the boat, and our progress after leaving Tell Houm became so very slow, that we resolved to land, and walk the rest of the way. Our path over a green and flowery hillside brought us shortly to another very strange sight, at the spot where the town of Bethsaida is supposed to have stood. The only remains visible, to us at least, were those of a great aqueduct coming down from the hills; a number of stately arches were still standing, and water was still running plentifully in the channel, but it had burst the limits in which it was enclosed, and, forcing its way through many a cleft, leapt down in a perfectly lawless manner

to the deserted plain, and made its way to the
lake in countless little independent rivulets.
On an island in the midst of all these little
streams, was a small Bedouin encampment, from
which a few wild stalwart fellows came forward
to carry the ladies of the party over the water
for an infinitesimal gratuity. There was something in the mean black tents of these wander-
ers which seemed to give a yet more desolate
appearance to the spot; yet here too may have
been a flourishing city. Higher up, on the hills
overlooking the lake, a few scattered ruins are
supposed to mark the site of Chorazin; the whole
of the prosperous community that filled these
coasts is utterly gone, brushed away off the face of
the earth, so that it is difficult to tell even where
they once lived. There is something more terrible in the solitude here than in the sandy
wastes around the Dead Sea;—there, one may
feel that some awful visitation has come upon
the country, and its effects are still more or less
visible; but here, looking over the smiling landscape, with the pleasant grassy hills, and the
sun shining on the lake, it is appalling to think
that such utter destruction has come upon all

these great centres of life and activity,—and that it makes no difference. The grass is as green now, the sea and sky as blue, as in the days of their prosperity ; their history is simply a closed page, turned over and done with ; they are gone, and the place thereof knoweth them no more.

A singular contrast was presented when we turned the corner of the next headland, and came upon a neat little white house, with a well-ordered garden and a pleasant little trellised porch, under which a table was being spread for us. This was the property of the pioneer of the German colony which is to be founded here, a hospitable, friendly Badener, from the shores of the Lake of Constance. His delight at the arrival of strangers who could speak his language more or less, and who had come from his brethren of the Temple at Haifa, was great, and he insisted on making gratuitous additions to our store, of native and European delicacies, wine of Safed, and liqueur from far - away Interlaken. The arrangements for the German settlement were progressing slowly, it appeared ; but some difficulty may be expected in a land where,

though foreigners are permitted by law to buy
land from the natives, the natives are not
allowed to sell it to them. The establishment
of the colony, however, is a certainty, and may
have great consequences to the country round,
where a little energy and enterprise may completely change the face of affairs, and bring back
prosperity to the shores of the lake. We took a
cordial leave of our host, and a short walk along
a beautiful path cut in the rock just above the
water, brought us to our camp, which had been
set up at a pleasant grassy spot not far from
the shore of the lake, surrounded with bushes
of flowering oleander, which bore the name of
Ain-et-Tin, or the Fountain of the Fig-tree, in a
corner of the plain of Gennesareth.

Next morning, with great regret, we had to
turn our backs upon the beautiful lake to pursue
our journey northward. The low hills above us
had first to be crossed, from which we got some
beautiful views backward over the lake and forward over the upper valley of the Jordan, along
which our journey would lie for the next two
days. It forms a broad and fairly flat plain, partly cultivated, partly used for pasture, but, except

for a few groups of rude Bedouin huts, almost entirely uninhabited.

On the hill we first crossed, but at some distance from the lake, we came across a ruinous khan, called for some reason the Khan of Joseph, which is used by passing travellers, though it does not look inviting, and is perhaps not more dilapidated than most khans in this country. Some considerable way further, when we had got down into the valley, the little Jewish colony of Rosetta—one of those which have been started under the auspices of the French branch of the Rothschild family—was pointed out to us, up on the hillside on the western slope of the valley, by a courteous Arab gentleman journeying on his own affairs—and on a lovely little black mare—who gave us what was no doubt an exhaustive account of the place, by which our ignorance of the language again prevented us from profiting. With these exceptions, from the time we lost sight of the Sea of Galilee till we reached Banyas on the second day, there was nothing to be seen but the primitive erections of the Bedouins, consisting usually of three low mud walls and a black canvas roof,

one side being left open. One of their villages,
if it could be called so, was established on the
site of an old Roman mining station, from which
a strange group of gaunt ill-favoured girls—the
Bedouin women seem to be uniformly ugly—
draped in the queer dark-blue garments of their
race, rushed out upon us with much shrill
chattering to offer for sale some Roman lamps
and other curiosities picked up about the place.
The incidents of the road were many. Occasionally we would meet an Arab party on their
travels, sometimes a dangerous-looking group
of men, armed to the teeth, and beautifully
mounted, but painfully harmless in demeanour,
passing what would once have been a rich prize
with no sign of notice but the solemn " *Mar-
haba !* " ("Welcome!") once uttered by every
member of the party: or at other times, a whole
family travelling together, the father either
mounted or on foot, with a gun slung round
his body, and a reed spear with a metal point,
some ten feet long, in his hand ; the women in a
little kind of tent on the back of a donkey, in
which two could sit, one on each side, to keep
the balance true ; and the children stowed away

somewhere about the beasts — in the saddle-bags, or the holsters, or whatever came handy. Certainly it was from the oddest places that we could see the little unkempt heads protruded, with cries of "*Bakshish, bakshish !*" apparently intended rather as a friendly greeting than with any hope of receiving anything. There is a story in Herodotus of an Egyptian king who had two children carefully isolated from their birth, to see what language they would evolve from their own consciousness, having heard nothing spoken. The first word they said was *bekos*, which was found to be the ancient Phrygian for "bread"; whereupon the Phrygian language was rather hastily pronounced to be the oldest language in the world. My experience in the East has convinced me that the king was mistaken, and that the word was *bakshish*, the first word which an Egyptian, or, for the matter of that, a Syrian baby, would naturally use, without requiring any mother or nurse to teach it.

Our first halting - place was at a place called Ain-el-Mellahah (the Fountain of the Pavement), in the neighbourhood of the Waters of Merom. The camp itself stood on firm ground, but the centre of the valley was of a very marshy character, even in our immediate neighbourhood. Perhaps this accounted in some degree for the plague of flies with which we were troubled. There had been much wind a little before sunset, at which we grumbled, and our dragoman told us it would drop at sunset, but we should be worse off then, for the flies would come. His prophecy proved perfectly true : at sunset the wind suddenly dropped, and the next moment everything about us—we were at dinner—was black with flies. Plates, glasses, knives, everything was covered with an infinity of tiny flies, who kept constantly increasing in number till we gave up our meal in despair and made a rush for the open air. Pharaoh himself cannot have suffered much more. The view of Mount Hermon from this point was magnificent, nor did we ever again see it nearly as well, though we had to beat about its sides for some time to come. Next day we still kept along the valley of the Jordan, and made our mid-day halt by one of its sources, where the round green knoll of the Cadi (Tell-el-Kadi) marks the

site of the ancient Dan, the northernmost point
of Israel in Old Testament days. An hour's
ride further through the thickets of oaks of
Bashan, which abound by the head-waters of
Jordan, brought us to Banyas, a beautiful little
village nestling right under the majestic Hermon,
the site of the ancient Cæsarea Philippi, and the
furthest place to which our Lord is known to
have come according to the names given in the
Gospel narratives : I believe, however, that not
only is the Transfiguration now generally considered to have taken place upon Mount Hermon—which would be a little farther north—
but that He is even supposed to have been at
or near Damascus. To this favoured spot it has
been given to have all the warmth and sunshine
of the south, together with that wealth of wood
and water which is generally reserved as a consolation for the colder north. Another of the
sources of the Jordan rises here, under a great
beetling mass of rock, in which a few shell-
shaped niches with inscriptions over them show
all that remains of a once great temple of Pan.
There is something almost comic in the piety of
these inscriptions in such a place, though the

H

surroundings are certainly such as Pan would have loved, the little river stealing away among the trees, and the prospect of the broad green valley stretching away to the south. Above the rocks a little beyond, a little white mosque looks complacently over the land in which, after so many vicissitudes, its religion has got the upper hand, while the hill to the back of the village is covered with the ruins of a crusading fortress. It is not only poor Pan's dead and forgotten religion that has faded out of the country before the fierce devotees of the little white mosque.

We were now on the very outskirts of Palestine, and the most interesting part of our journey was over. A day's scrambling over the lower slopes of Hermon in very bad weather brought us to the plain on the other side of the range in which Damascus lies. Our first resting-place was in a very windy valley on the banks of a branch of the Pharpar, opposite the village of Beit Jenn: while on the second night our tents were pitched on a knoll above the pretty little town of Kattana, the traditional site of St Paul's conversion. We had been

travelling by very easy stages, as we had a
mule-palanquin with us which could not go very
fast or very far in one day. At Kattana civilisation met us in the shape of a landau, in which
we had an agonising drive to Damascus over an
appalling parody of a road. Here also we had
to take an affecting farewell of our numerous
retainers, with the exception of our dragoman,
who accompanied us as far as Constantinople.
The praise of other men's servants is seldom
interesting to the most indulgent reader, or I
would willingly write the panegyric of all these
worthy persons, collectively or in detail,—of
Hamet, the swift-footed, the untiring, who performed the whole journey on foot, and always
arrived first at the camping-ground; of Rashid,
the helpful, the music-loving, always at hand
when anything was wanted, and under all circumstances singing to himself the same monotonous Arab song; of Georgy, the simple and
blundering, who officiated as a kind of under-
waiter or steward, and seemed always in disgrace
with his chief, the consequential Ibrahim; of
Hadj Hassan—who had made the pilgrimage to
Mecca, and wore a strip of green in his turban

in commemoration of the fact — and of his donkey. The donkey especially: he was a beast of an aspiring mind, and when the pace was not too severe for him, he loved to walk at the head of the party. Having once attained this desirable position, he would resort to every kind of device to prevent any one passing him. It was quite a lesson in race-riding to try and get ahead of him, having to creep up to his shoulder without attracting his attention, and then to "come" at exactly the right moment, before he could rush across your path and shoulder you back. Usually, in the East, the first place appears to be accorded to the donkey without dispute, for almost every string of camels that we met was headed by a small grave donkey, who had the end of the rope which passed from one to another of the great beasts behind. But enough of donkeys; as old Gerard Legh says, " I could write much of this beast, but that it would be thought it were to mine own glory."

VII.

THE early Mohammedans thought Damascus an earthly representation of Paradise ; more modern visitors say that to realise this idea you must have been born in the desert. Certainly the approach to the city is extremely beautiful—perhaps, with the exception of Banyas, the prettiest, or rather the pleasantest, bit of scenery we have seen in Palestine. Here, again, we have the fresh green trees and the cool gurgling water, in strong contrast to the barren hills on the western side—the end of the Hermon range— or the yet more sterile country to the east, which is, indeed, the beginning of the great Syrian desert. There is something very refreshing in the long stretch of the famous Damascus gardens, or, more properly speaking,

orchards, outside the city ; but they are not yet
quite in their fullest beauty.   Passing beyond
them, we come to a still more beautiful scene.
The road lies along the southern side of the
depression in which Damascus lies.   A little
stream of water, in an old Roman aqueduct cut
in the rock, flows by its side with a pleasant
murmur ; while the valley below us gradually
opens out, a grassy plain divided by the clear
blue waters of the Abana, with the countless
domes and minarets of the city beginning to
show in the distance.   As we come down upon
the valley, and cross the Abana, we come upon
the beautiful Mosque of the Dervishes, a great
dome between two tall minarets surrounded by
others of varying size, which reminded us irre-
sistibly of the singular Church of St Antonio
at Padua.   Unfortunately it is rather too new
to have served as a model for the Santo, or
we might think that some Venetian explorer
had brought back a sketch of it; it is also
extremely improbable that the Mohammedan
architect has taken his model from Italy, so
we must decide that the resemblance is acci-
dental, if, indeed, it does not prove to be

imaginary. The mosque, at any rate, has the advantage over the Christian church of standing in a cool enclosure, shaded by fine trees, of a size that we have not seen in Palestine. There was an exuberance of foliage and verdure on every side of us as we drove along the river-bank into the city.

The wonders of Damascus are very difficult to expound to others, the greatest wonder seeming to us to consist in our being there at all. There is not very much to see, as compared with some other places; but it should take one half a life-time to see it. The whole city seems so completely what it ought to be, such a perfect type of all that is strange and mysterious in Eastern life. The crowd in the bazaars is just as we have fancied it to be since we first read the 'Arabian Nights,' if there ever was a time when we read them first. The bazaars are always the first thing that a visitor to Damascus thinks of. My principal recollection is of a pleasant little street that led to them. I forget whether it was called a bazaar itself; but it was not covered in, and it had shops on one side, and on the other great trees, the

hollow trunk of one of which was the dwelling-
place of a dervish. I believe it was also on
these trees that the ringleaders of the 1860
massacres were hanged, which is not a very
cheery association for any one. Among the
houses were at least two mosques, such as
are to be found all over the place, with little
unpretending entrances, which do not attract the
attention, only one of the open arches of the
court giving a glimpse of the beauty of the
interior. At the further end was a more pre-
tentious place of worship, with a very fine
doorway decorated with coloured marbles, and
a minaret of fine carved stone-work. Here we
came into the bazaars proper, a series of un-
paved streets, roofed in at the top, which
occupy the principal part of the city. They
run in all directions, but through the midst of
them goes the stately "street which is called
Straight," little changed, no doubt, from what
it was in St Paul's time, a broad straight road,
traversing the city from east to west, and
covered in like the others. The wares are of
every conceivable kind, each trade having a
division to itself. There is the Shoemaker's

Bazaar and the Harness Bazaar, the Gold-
workers' and the Silversmiths', the Silk Bazaar,
the Cloth Bazaar, the Bakers' and the Pastry-
cooks', and many others, each with a separate
street, in which no other trade is conducted.
Among the most curious is the Bazaar of Sales,
where second-hand articles of all kinds are sold
by peripatetic salesmen, who push their way
about, shrieking the amount offered by the last
bidder for the wares they are carrying. The
shops are in most cases little more than small
cupboards open to the public, with just room
for the merchant to sit in a corner; but the
richer traders often keep their stores out of sight.
A little obscure entrance down a dirty passage
leads suddenly into one of the beautiful Damascus
interiors, a cool inner court, planted with lemon
and orange trees, with a fountain in the centre,
and a recess fitted with a divan at one end, in
which the merchant's family are luxuriously
reclining. The traveller, under these circumstances, will probably go completely off his head,
and fall a willing victim to the persuasive offers
of the courteous merchant. But no doubt he
has expected to spend his money at Damascus,

and if he has an honest dragoman, skilled in
bargaining, will find the treasures offered him
not dear. Should he prefer to buy nothing,
he can find almost the same things for sale in
London,—at three times the price.

So much for the sellers; but who could give
anything like an adequate picture of the buyers
or the passers-by ?—an ever-changing crowd of
men and horses, camels and donkeys, from
every corner of the East. Arabs, Kurds, Druses,
Circassians, Negroes, every conceivable variety
of Eastern humanity elbowing each other along,
dodging the projecting loads of passing camels,
or hastily crushed into a corner by the approach
of a carriage almost large enough to fill up
the road itself, with a load of infidel sight-seers,
whose mere presence is an insult to the feelings
of the true believer. It adds a certain piquancy
to the general interest of the scene to know that
the unbelieving visitor is really a source of
fanatical hatred to the great mass of the population. Only thirty years ago, Damascus was
the scene of a fearful massacre of Christians,
and the offenders, it is hard for us to believe,
were those same kindly hospitable Druses we

had fraternised with on Mount Carmel. We had expected to forgather once more here with the Druse sheikhs of Daliyeh, who were called to Damascus on business about this time; but they had, unfortunately, been obliged to leave before our arrival. We were inclined to hope that there might be some mistake in the stories told us of 1860. It is certainly strange that Druses and Mohammedans, who hold each other in abomination, should have joined hands even against the hated Maronites.[1]

The principal sight of Damascus is the great mosque, which is magnificent. It has once been a Christian church, and still retains some of its characteristics, its form being that of a great nave with two lines of pillars running along it, and one or two graceful little shrines interspersed, one, I believe, supposed to contain the head of St John the Baptist, known here by the uneuphonious name of Neby Yahyah. There even remains over one of its great gates, now

[1] M. Elisée Reclus, in his magnificent work, the 'Nouvelle Géographie Universelle,' says, "On accusa les Druzes d'être les auteurs de ces exterminations en masse, mais ils n'y prirent qu'une faible part; les principaux coupables furent les soldats turcs, réguliers et irréguliers."—Vol. ix. p. 755.

disused and ruinous, and only attainable by a
staircase communicating with the bazaar of the
(Christian) silversmiths, the Greek inscription,
set up by its original owners: " Thy kingdom,
O Christ, is an everlasting kingdom, and thy
dominion endureth throughout all generations."
Such inscriptions are usually erased with great
care by the Mohammedans. One or two may
also be found, however, in the mosque of St
Sophia at Constantinople. The court of the
mosque is a singularly beautiful one, and con-
tains some exquisite little cupolas, used as
storehouses for the sacred books, while out
of the court opens the splendid mausoleum
of Saladin. The mosque was crowded, when
we visited it, with motley groups of men of
various nationalities—a few engaged in their
devotions, but most of them simply loafing or
chatting in little groups. It was the month of
Ramadan, the most sacred month of the year to
the pious Mohammedan, and I have no doubt our
intrusion was regarded as particularly untimely
and unwarrantable. It appeared that our escort
—consisting of four Turkish soldiers, with a non-
commissioned officer in command, a *cavasse* from

the Consulate, and two or three dragomans, for it was a large mixed party — were a little nervous about the chance of some insult being offered to us. In the month of Ramadan the Moslem law, among other regulations, requires true believers to fast from sunrise to sunset, and fasting naturally makes men savage. Nothing occurred, however, though we were afterwards told that insulting remarks were made by the men who crowded round us while one of the soldiers was struggling to turn the key in the rusty wards of the lock of Saladin's mausoleum. This, it appears, is a very sacred spot, which the wretched infidel is not always allowed to visit. As we did not understand the insults, we remained most stolidly unaffected by them.

The inhabitants of Damascus have the reputation of being the most fanatical Mohammedans out of Arabia, with the exception perhaps of those of Hebron. They are also, fortunately for the traveller, very conservative in all things, and offer a strenuous resistance to the encroachments of infidel refinements. But for this feeling the city would not be so entirely and delightfully oriental; the few carriages are almost the only things which remind one of the nineteenth century, and considering the nature of the crowd in the streets, they are a sufficient advantage, from the point of view of convenience, to make up for their want of keeping with the surroundings. The driver should be instructed to take particular care not to run over any of the many dogs, whose lot is already hard enough in this city of the faithful. If you do happen to hurt one of the poor beasts, the nearest representative of that noble species, man, will very probably give it a kick on the injured part to show a true believer's loathing for an unclean animal. I may perhaps take the opportunity here to record a protest against the inconsiderate abuse which is so often lavished upon the dog of Palestine—who is really a most estimable beast—even by Christian travellers. He is certainly not pretty to look at, but to class him at once, as many people do, as a "horrid wild animal" is merely the injustice of ignorance. The Palestine dog —in every case I have ever come across— is very sensible of kindness, and eagerly and pitifully grateful for it. His faults are the

effect of the abuse of man's power over him;
one might almost parody the axiom of the
Galician novelist, Franzos, about the Jews, and
say that every land has the dogs that it deserves.

From Damascus to the coast at Beyrout
there is that most precious of rarities in Syria,
a really good road, made by the engineers of
a French carriage company in 1863. That
those French engineers may be rewarded according to their works is the earnest prayer of the
thankful traveller. The scenery through which
it passes is generally pretty, and at times very
grand; but the very magnificence of the surroundings shows us what difficulties must have
been surmounted before the road could be made.
We left Damascus by the right bank of the
Abana, or Barada as it is now called, as we
approached it by the left, and followed the river
for a considerable way towards its source in the
Anti-Lebanon range. The lower part of the
Wady Barada is of a peaceful character, full of
soft green foliage, and dotted here and there
with white buildings, the country-houses of
wealthy Damascus merchants. The scenery
grew grander as we got further on; the char-

acter of the gorge changed ; wild bare cliffs
rose on either side of us, and we seemed to be
in the heart of a most inhospitable desert, but
still, by the side of the little river there was the
same luxuriance of vegetation of every kind.
This, however, did not last very long, for the
road left the stream and entered another valley
where the rock-walls were as imposing, but the
centre of the valley was no longer as an oasis in
the desert, but rather a part of the desert itself.
The cliffs here are grouped in such fantastic
masses that one wonders that there should be
no wild Mohammedan legend to account for
their formation, especially as the neighbourhood
is full of sacred associations to the Mussulman,
reaching to the earliest times. Adam is believed to have been made out of the red earth
of a spur of Mount Hermon overlooking Damascus. The rocks of the Anti-Lebanon range are
just of the kind that tradition loves to represent
as the remains of some mythical hold,

> " Piled by the hand of giants
> For godlike kings of old."

But at least no such story was told us.   On

the desert plateau here, we were informed, the troops at Damascus hold manœuvres from time to time; but this information was unexciting.

The road became less interesting for a while, and a tiresome series of ascents and descents had to be gone through before we had made our way through the fastnesses of the Anti-Lebanon range and got our first view of the central plain. This great and fertile valley, called by the ancients Cœle-Syria, or Hollow Syria, and now known by the almost equivalent Arab name of Bukeia, stretches away for more than fifty miles between the Lebanon and Anti-Lebanon ranges, and is watered by the river Litany, which flows down it to its southern extremity, some twenty miles north-west of Banyas, and thereafter, forcing its way through a narrow rocky gorge, flows into the sea a little to the north of Tyre. The Bukeia is one of the richest districts in Syria, and its smiling corn-fields and fresh green pasture were very pleasant in our eyes. On the further side of the plain we halted at Storah, where the road to Baalbek—which, unfortunately, we had no time to visit—breaks off, and where there was

I

then only a small and rather primitive inn, which called itself a hotel. Now, I believe, the hotel at Storah is one of the best in Palestine. From here the road began to wind up the bare eastern slope of Lebanon. The scenery here was rugged, and rather imposing at places, with fine views backwards on the plain, and the Anti-Lebanon and Hermon ranges beyond; but this was nothing to compare with the grand view of the sea, and the valleys beneath, and the great Lebanon chain stretching away to the north, which came before us when we had got to the further side of the ridge. Almost on the very top we passed a singular group of three or four eagles and a couple of vultures— truly loathsome creatures these last, with their ringed necks, bald heads, and cruel beaks—apparently deliberating as to what they should do, whether in the way of sport or other business we could not tell. We had hoped that eagles would have kept better company. The road all the way down remains interesting, but the view gradually narrows down to very little beyond the sea, and an unbroken view of the sea is never to me personally a source of intoxicating delight. The entrance to the town of Beyrout cannot be called interesting, but this is not out of keeping with the character of the town itself.

The only point of view from which Beyrout could possibly be considered interesting is from the contrast it forms to the conservative system we had observed at Damascus. Beyrout is nothing if not progressive. All innovations that come from the westward are acceptable in its eyes; nor does it ever think twice about the advisability of leaving the ancient way when this has once been suggested. The result would hardly be gratifying to the most ardent apostle of progress. There are certainly streets of such an advanced character that in them carriages are not necessarily instruments of torture, but this is almost the only substantial advantage that I could observe. For the rest, Beyrout gives one the idea of a sort of parody of a French seaside resort, of which it reproduces all the least attractive attributes. The same may be said of many coast towns in the Levant. The country round is rather pretty, and the aspect of the town from the sea is pleasing enough, while the views of the Lebanon range

—spurs of which run down almost to the shore
of St George's Bay, a little north of Beyrout—
are very fine indeed. The mosque is an old
Crusaders' church, but Christians are very seldom allowed to visit it. Otherwise there is
absolutely no interest attaching to the place,
except that St George is said to have killed
his dragon on the shores of the bay which
bears his name. The contest between Perseus
and his monster took place near Jaffa, so that
there seems to have been good sport with
dragons along this coast in bygone days. They
are not, however, to be met with frequently
now, and the sportsman of the present day
must content himself with smaller game. There
are wild boars in plenty in the lower valley of
the Jordan,—to kill which is an act of charity
to the native proprietors,—and Mount Carmel
simply swarms with porcupines.

VIII.

THE BALANCE OF POWER IN PALESTINE.

IT is impossible to visit Palestine without being
struck by the unanimous feeling manifested by
its many different sects and divisions of some
approaching change, which is vaguely expected
to relieve in a way as yet undefined the evils
of that unfavoured land. The sentiment is no
doubt strongest among the Christian sects, who
detest each other with a hatred passing the hate
of the Mohammedan, and who look forward to
important results ensuing upon the great European contest which is expected to come off some
time within the present generation, and must, in
their opinion, have a great effect on the future
of Palestine. Diplomatists in general are apt
to make no very great account of this corner of
the earth, though its value, even from the prosaic

point of view of fertility, is considerable; and
the matter-of-fact statesman is a little scornful
of the sentimental longings to possess the land
of so many sacred associations, when compared
with questions of practical politics. Yet the
most superficial traveller to the Holy Land can
see that the sentiment thus excited in various
forms among the followers of various creeds, is
as formidable in its way as the superstition
which animated the Ghazis of Afghanistan or
the Dervishes of the Soudan. The people who
talk and plot about the future ownership of the
Holy Land are no idle dreamers. Religious enthusiasts they may be, but their views are emi-
nently practical; and each looks to the increase
of the temporal dominion of the State which
protects him as indicating his ascendancy over
his spiritual adversaries. It is a singular effect
of visiting the places where the Gospel of Peace
was first preached, that it appears to arouse
among many of the least excitable of men a
kind of appetite for an internecine religious
war such as, happily, has rarely been seen in
this world; but there are many profoundly religious people who regard the tolerance of other

ideas than their own as a sign of indifference to the truth. The Greek Christian in the Holy Land regards the Latin in almost the same light as the follower of Mohammed, though in his own country he might think nothing at all of the difference of creed. The followers of one sect are in the eyes of all others mischievous heretics, the propriety of whose mere presence on the sacred soil is doubtful, and is reasonably the cause of many most un-Christian conflicts. All these troubles, however, they believe will be removed when Russia is victorious and the Greek Church shall inherit the earth; or when the supremacy of France is established, and the hands of the Latin Catholics are strengthened; or in such other cases as the various remaining religious parties desire. Nor are the adherents of the various Churches either reluctant to engage in the conflict, or despondent as to their power of letting loose the dogs of war when the proper time comes.

It is no great cause of wonder that all alike are dissatisfied with the present condition of Palestine. It would be a bold statement to assert that there is no worse governed province

in the Turkish dominions; but its condition is
at least sufficiently grievous to excite the as-
tonishment and indignation even of the chance
visitor, unless he has already some experience
of the benefits of Ottoman rule in other parts.
The difficulty of getting official sanction for any
kind of projected improvement is one of the
principal mysteries to the inexperienced; yet
much of this may be accounted for by the short
and uncertain tenure of office enjoyed by the
various governors and under-governors of the
country.   There is really no time to think of
anything that does not bring in money at once.
Palestine is divided under the last arrangement
longitudinally into two parts: the less visited
half, east of the Jordan, is subject to the Walee
of Damascus; the western half, including almost
all the scenes described, to the Governor of
Beyrout, next to whom come the two Mutaserifs
or lieutenant-governors, as we may call them, of
northern and southern Palestine, whose respective
headquarters are at Acre and Jerusalem.   Beneath them again are the smaller potentates, rejoicing in the title of Kaimakam, whose principal
duty is to collect a sufficient amount of taxes for

the superior officer to remit to the central Government, with a trifling margin for his trouble, and perhaps a small extra contribution to eke out the scanty salary allotted to an official who is known to have sufficient opportunities for helping himself. Among these are undoubtedly some officials—possibly many—who are honest and intelligent, and sincerely desire the welfare of the province committed to their charge. But it must be remembered that even the Governor of Damascus is liable to be removed at short notice, and rarely retains his command for a whole year, and that when there is a change in the head of the government, all the underlings are likely to be turned out of office also. "Every man for himself" is therefore not unnaturally the maxim of the smaller authorities at any rate; if their tenure of office is to be short, it must be made all the more profitable while it does last, and the unhappy peasantry must pay the piper. The people of the country are patient enough; indeed, any attempt at resistance or remonstrance only brings further evils on their devoted heads. The Kaimakam is absolute in his small way, and there is no hope of making a stand against him or his myrmidons. The Turkish soldier himself is, in the enlightened nineteenth century, an exact reproduction of the *lanzknecht* of the middle ages; undaunted in battle, — where his services are often held to outweigh all his misconduct at other seasons,— but in time of peace an absolute pest to the country, with an insatiable appetite for pleasure and gain, utterly unscrupulous how he procures them, obedient to no authority but that of his immediate military superior,—and not to him when there is a chance of a successful mutiny. To such administrators of the law, the peasant has no power to refuse anything, happy if only the extortioner may be content with all he has, and does not march himself off to forced military service as a penalty for not having more to give.

To such dominion, however, the peasant is accustomed,—as eels are to being skinned,—and probably would not even wish for a change of rulers, which would seem to him but an exchange of tyrants. But the stranger who comes into Palestine,—especially if he wishes to settle, as foreigners continue to do in spite of the resistance of the Turkish Government,—detests and resents this obnoxious system ; and, if he be in the slightest way inclined to entertain political views as to the future of Palestine, it is almost impossible that he should not say to himself, " Would it not be Christian charity to relieve these poor people from the intolerable burdens laid upon them ? It is naturally objectionable that the Holy Land should be in the hands of an infidel Power, but it might be borne if that Power's rule were even ordinarily just. But here we have a Government that is obviously unfit for such a charge. Is it not our duty to take it out of their hands ? " I am not to be supposed to indorse such an opinion : I merely represent it as it occurs to many. Timid and feeble, even to imbecility, in its foreign relations, and brutally tyrannical at home, the Turkish Government wilfully alienates the support, even of those who are most willing to make allowances. It needs no long experience to understand the two categories into which the Sublime Porte divides those who have any dealings with it : (i.) enemies —*i.e.*, persons to be feared—cringe to them ; and (ii.) friends—*videlicet*, good-natured fools—take advantage of their folly. It is no very great

wonder if the latter are often disgusted, while
the pretensions of the former grow constantly
greater. As it happens, two of the most
influential parties in Palestine are respec-
tively led by the two Powers most dangerous
to Turkey, whose principal consolation must
be that the nations in question, however
united upon other subjects, remain and must
continue deadly enemies in the Holy Land.
In this fact lies for the present the safety of
the Turkish rule in Palestine, as the most ardent
enthusiasts for the rescue of the holy places from
Mohammedan hands have the one great natural
barrier between them. The lion will lie down
with the lamb long before the Greek and Latin
Churches will join hands even against a common foe.

The population of Palestine may amount to
some three hundred thousand souls, of whom
about two-thirds are at present Mohammedans.
It is not, however, in this Moslem population
that the Turkish Government will find any
zealous defenders of the existing *régime*. The
fellaheen of Palestine, who form the bulk of the
Mohammedan element, are not without good

points, but they are by no means warlike. Nor
are they in the least likely to fight either for the
Government they live under or for the religion
they profess. The peasantry of Palestine are
believed to be the direct descendants of the
ancient Canaanites, and have been hewers of
wood and drawers of water since the time of
Joshua. For three thousand years they have
been accustomed to be ruled, with varying de-
grees of cruelty, by alien masters professing
various religions, Jewish, Pagan, Christian, and
Mohammedan, to each of which they have con-
formed in turn. But these alien creeds have
probably never taken any very strong hold on
their spirit; and there may be detected, under
the veneer of Islamism which covers them at
present, remnants of ceremonies and superstitions
which take their origin from some very ancient
heathen worship which they have never aban-
doned. To people such as these it can matter
very little from a religious point of view whether
their rulers be Moslem or Christian ; while, as
regards material prosperity, their lot would certainly be easier under the rule of a civilised Power.
It is not certain whether they are aware of this

last fact, but they must know at least that they could hardly exchange for the worse.

The more warlike Arabs of the south could not probably be counted upon much more than the passive fellaheen of the plains in a struggle where Turkey seemed likely to get the worst of it. There is no love for the house of Osman among Arab nations. The Sultan is indeed the commander of the faithful, so long as he is established at Constantinople ; but should there be any chance of his losing the immense prestige attaching to the possession of dominions in Europe,—as is not improbable, if the Turkish Government continue the sagacious and enlightened policy of giving the cat the cream to keep,—there are princes in Arabia of as sacred a line as Abdul Hamid himself, who will be set up in opposition and will prove very formidable rivals. Let the Sultan be once driven across the Bosphorus, said one who had studied the Moslem populations deeply, and all Arabia will revolt. There is little material for the Turkish Government to count upon there. It may be mentioned, at the same time, that the proximity of Arabia would be one of the greatest dangers to be provided against by any European Power which could possess itself of Palestine.

So far I have attempted to show three things. In the first place, that there is among all sects in the country—with the exception perhaps of the timid native cultivator—a general expectation and desire of some change in the government of Palestine; secondly, that that government as at present existing is radically bad, and that any change from it would be to the advantage of the people; and, thirdly, that in case of a contest for the possession of the country, it is not probable that the inhabitants would make any stand on behalf of their present rulers. I think that these combined facts entitle us to look to a change in the affairs of Palestine which may possibly be very near at hand.   Unless the system of government can be entirely reformed, I fear that every visitor to Palestine will even be inclined to hope that such a change may be very near indeed.   But this is hardly a profitable subject for speculation; a more practical inquiry would be, What other lot is possible for Palestine; and what advantages or disadvantages are implied thereby ?

Supposing, then, that Palestine is no longer under Turkish rule, it may be said at once that no other Mohammedan Power is likely to establish its supremacy there. No doubt the Arabs of the borders might be inclined to make fight for the possession of the Holy City, and might, from time to time, especially in an age when Mahdis are fashionable, make serious attacks upon Palestine, with the support of the stronger and more fanatical tribes of Arabia itself. But I cannot consider this as more than a danger against which the occupants of Palestine would be bound to make provision, and probably would make quite adequate provision. There would be frontier troubles constantly recurring, at least for the first twenty or thirty years, but it is within the resources of civilisation to overcome such disturbances. Leaving Mohammedan rule aside, we find apparently no less than four possible future conditions for Palestine. It may be occupied by any one of three European Powers, Russia, France, or England,—no other nation has a sufficient interest in the country to have any claim,—or it may be formed into a little State by itself. We may now consider the re-

spective advantages of each of these conditions
in detail.

It is natural to consider first the claims of the
Greek Church, which has much the most numerous following of all Christian sects in Palestine.
To the Greeks and the kindred sects all hope
for the future centres in Russia, and that very
energetic Power shows no intention of disappointing the confidence thus put in her. Neither
her diplomatic nor her civil servants are allowed
to lose sight of Palestine.   The Greek Patriarch
of Jerusalem is, through the exertion of Russian
influence at Constantinople, practically the
nominee of the Czar. Pilgrimages from Russia
receive encouragement and even pecuniary
support from the State, and the Imperial
Government is never slow to point out to the
pious and stalwart pilgrims it sends forth the
many advantages, spiritual and temporal, of
settling in the Holy Land.   The Russian Christian, once settled, feels perfect and well-warranted
confidence in the power of his Government to
meet all objections on the part of Turkey to
his presence or his behaviour.   The amount of
interest taken in the affairs of Palestine at St

K

Petersburg may be estimated by the fact that Russian officials have even intervened in protection of the Jews of their own nation, whose treatment by the authorities at home can hardly be described as paternal. In view of all these facts, it cannot be doubted that Russia would be glad to possess herself of Palestine, which would probably be of more political importance to her than to any other nation. The possession of Jerusalem would indeed add so enormously to the prestige of Russia—at least among Slav races and in the Greek Church—that it is for that reason highly inexpedient that she should ever be permitted to acquire it. Of other reasons for and against a Russian occupation of Palestine, we may say that the country would, in Russian hands, probably be better off than it is now ; the peasantry, whose submissive character would admirably suit Muscovite landlords, would not be quite so harshly treated, and there would undoubtedly be a great deal done in the matter of roads and other public works, of which it is difficult to overrate the importance. But the present intolerant spirit existing in the Greek Church of Palestine—as in other Churches too, unfortunately — would not be restrained but encouraged, and it is probable that pilgrims of any other shade of belief would find a great many new difficulties thrown in their way, and the Latin Church would be practically extinguished. Now, one of the first points in the readjustment of the government of Palestine— if there is sufficient reason for a change at all —must be the stipulation that pilgrims of all nations and beliefs have equal liberty of access to the sacred places they wish to visit. This is the first general objection to the Russian supremacy; others arise from the general belief that though the peasantry would be better treated and the country turned to better account by Russia than by Turkey, yet a more civilised Power would be better qualified to take charge of people and country than either. So much for general reasons; from the point of view of England, it would be absolutely impossible to tolerate the presence of Russia so near the Suez Canal under any circumstances whatever.

The Latin Church—or, as we in Europe are accustomed to call it, the Roman Catholic Church—looks to France as its deliverer. It

has made great progress in Palestine of late
years, owing to the unceasing work of the
Franciscan and other Latin monks, and is now
more near to equality with the Greek Church
than has ever yet been the case. Strangely
enough, in view of the anti-religious attitude
taken up of late years by the home Government, there is not only a great interest taken
by France in the ecclesiastical affairs of the
Holy Land, but the French consuls are chosen
principally with regard to their individual piety.
The result may, perhaps, be a little trying to
some of the gentlemen themselves, as the Latin
Catholicism of Palestine is very catholic indeed,
and includes a variety of strange sects, whose
practices cannot commend themselves to a strict
observer of Catholic principles as understood in
Europe. " The French consul-general at Beyrout," said Laurence Oliphant, "goes to Mass
on Easter Sunday with the Roman Catholics.
On Easter Monday he attends Mass with the
Maronites, and on Tuesday he worships with
the Melchites, thus dividing his favours equally,
and patronising with great impartiality any
heresies he may happen to come across."

Such impartiality is, however, a most suitable characteristic of a Power which aims at ruling in Palestine; and it is in a great measure owing to the fact that France has not the same ecclesiastical character or connection between Church and State as Russia has, and could hardly, without inconsistency, allow of any religious persecution, that many people are inclined to think French dominion in Palestine not undesirable. That France has long had an eye upon the rich province of Syria is well known; and no existing Power would be more qualified to take it in hand and develop its resources. In the memorandum drawn up by General Gordon after the Treaty of San Stefano, embodying the best arrangement of the situation that he could see, Egypt was to be given to England, and Syria to France, who would thus be equally interested with England in checking the further advance of Russia to the East. Of course, Syria could not be given to France unless Egypt was definitely in the hands of England, and, perhaps, Tripoli held by Italy; but in such a case there are many advantages that might arise to both countries by such a redistribution

of the shores of the Mediterranean. To secure
so substantial an advantage to a Power which
England has always wished to count among her
best friends would be, from the point of view
of general convenience, a wise and statesmanlike
measure, and one which would undoubtedly be
popular among her Majesty's subjects. The
public works necessary in Palestine would be
soon and well done in the hands of so energetic and civilised a nation; the country would
thrive generally; and full religious liberty, we
may be assured, would be allowed to Christians of all creeds. It does seem almost the
most hopeful future that could be designed for
Palestine; and it is a great pity that we should
be obliged to reject it. But it is not possible to believe that the tolerance of France
would be absolutely universal; and what injustice was done would fall upon those whom
we are bound to protect. Without counting
the probable ill treatment of the German
settlers—who have a Government of their own
to look after them—there can be little doubt
that French rule in Palestine would mean the
extermination of the fine Druse nation. The

French bear them a grudge already for having slipped through their fingers in 1861, when, but for the intervention of England, Napoleon III. would have made an end of them once for all. It was just the kind of sweeping measure that would go to the heart of a sovereign who played so consistently to the gallery. Even if the French authorities nowadays were not inclined to initiate any severe measures against the Druses—and it is not probable that they would do so without a more or less decent pretext—the Maronites, who are among the most powerful adherents of the Latin Church, and the bitterest foes of the Druses, would be sure to precipitate matters. It would not be easy to utterly destroy the gallant Druses, who have so often repulsed the unprovoked attacks of unprincipled Turkish governors on the rich lands of the Hauran; but France has done as hard and as cruel work already in Algeria. England, however, could not, with unstained honour, stand by and see the work of destruction done upon a people who love her and put trust in her good-will. The impossibility of providing against such measures being taken in a remote and little-visited district seems to me in itself a sufficient reason why England should resist the establishment of French supremacy in Syria.

The great Powers of Palestine are, after the Mohammedans, the Greek and Latin Churches, who would probably consider themselves the only persons to be taken into account in a consideration of the future of the country. But there is besides these a remnant in Israel, made up of many various elements, but chiefly of Protestants, Jews, and Druses, who severally, and with no thought of action in common, look to the establishment of British rule in the Holy Land as the most hopeful manner of settling all difficulties. With the Protestants, whose numbers are very small, such aspirations are only natural; the Jews regard England as a Power in whose hands their interests are fairly safe, and are probably not unaware of the sentimental inclination to give back Palestine to the Jews, which is nowhere stronger than among us. As for the Druses, they have some slight memories of protection afforded at no great price

in time past, and a vague idea of some mysterious affinity which binds them to us, the two
together producing a feeling of attachment and
confidence which one would willingly do something to deserve. Probably no section of Palestine would, in time of war, have a more important voice in deciding its destinies than the
Druses ; their numbers are not very great, but
they contain the best fighting material to be
found in those parts, with the exception, perhaps,
of some select Bedouin tribes. I mention this
as showing that an attempt to extend British
rule over Palestine would be attended with
perhaps less difficulties, and require less vio-
lence, than any invasion by France or Russia.
Nor do I think that the people of the Holy
Land would have any call to complain of the
consequences of even annexation on the part
of England, much less of a British protectorate.
Energy, justice, and toleration are the things
wanted in Palestine, and these we humbly believe to be usually supplied in most of our
dependencies ; nor can I foresee any likelihood
of internal troubles were England to take charge
of the Holy Land—unless, indeed, the Anglican

element, which always shows such an astounding desire to fraternise with the Greek Church, as opposed to the less superstitious and less tyrannical Latin establishment, were allowed to push itself into the front rank.   But England has no desire to annex Palestine, nor indeed would she be suffered to do so without unanimous protests from many influential nationalities, whose susceptibilities it would be madness to offend in a cause which would bring no substantial advantage to the British people, and only enlist the sympathies of a comparatively small minority among them.

The establishment of a British protectorate is more within the range of practical politics. Unless following upon some European convulsion, even this would be a stronger step than our cautious rulers are apt to take, but all our suppositions are based upon some revolution in the affairs of the world as known to our politicians.   I should not myself expect to see such a measure, even as the consequence of a war which materially increased the power of Great Britain; but it might possibly be set up for a while to give some new form of government in Palestine a fair chance without molestation from external sources. Should the event of a European war leave the destinies of the Holy Land in our hands, much pressure would certainly be brought to bear on the Government to try the experiment of restoring the country to the Jews. It is a favourite dream among Englishmen this restoration of Palestine to its early conquerors, and it would certainly be very ardently advocated in such a case. For my part, I cannot believe that any such plan would succeed. It is extremely doubtful whether any Jewish community could be formed in these days at all fit to administer such a country as Palestine. They have, it is true, been in some cases successful as colonists; but a much higher and more difficult task would be imposed upon them in the case supposed. They must, to justify even the experiment, be qualified to stand alone when once restored to their old country; and what expectation can we have that they could do so? If their government required to be constantly bolstered up by extraneous assistance, it would not be worth the trouble and expense necessary to support it. It

is allowable, however, to suppose that a real
Jewish nation might be re-formed, capable of
standing by itself and defending itself against
all adversaries, and we may ask, Who would
profit by the establishment of such a power?
The country possibly, for there are no better
men of business than the Jews; the people not
probably, for Hebrew masters are not famed for
gentleness, and there would be no peerages to
be won by philanthropy there; while as for the
pilgrims,—a Jewish Government, strong enough
to be independent, would probably be more intolerant than the harshest Mohammedan ruler
that has yet been known.

There is, however, perhaps a chance that an
independent State might be set up in Palestine
which could take care of itself without being
offensive to others. It could only exist under
the sanction of the strongest guarantees from all
the Powers interested — say, England, France,
Germany, Russia, and such Mohammedan Power
or Powers as may be to the front at the time
when the question comes to be considered. It
is true that guarantees are of little value in our
days — perhaps they never were, though one

likes to think that there was once a time when nations kept more honourably to their engagements. Still Belgium has not yet been attacked in the forty odd years of its history. In the new State the utmost liberty must be accorded to all manner of creeds, of access to the sacred places, and exercise of their religion. Liberty to settle under some slight restrictions should be freely granted, and new colonists, for the first few years at least, easily admitted to the privileges of citizenship. There would, of course, be some danger of a manufactured majority, who would vote for the establishment of the protectorate, if not of the actual dominion of some foreign Power, but this might be easily guarded against. Money would be necessary, but capitalists should have little reluctance to make advances to a country so rich in natural resources. A considerable amount of public works, particularly in the line of roads—but not railways—and harbours would be imperative; but the expense thus incurred would be fully counterbalanced by the increased facilities for disposing of the plentiful and varied produce of the land. Coast defences might also be required, as a provision against a possible *coup-de-main*, but the guarantees of neutrality ought perhaps to make them unnecessary. The hardest matter in reality would be to protect the newly established State to the south, especially in the direction of Arabia, from which the most danger would be apprehended. The absence of a sufficient force to withstand any such attack would be a serious matter. In a few years it might be practicable to set on foot a serviceable militia force, with European officers, who might make a sufficient frontier guard, at least with the aid of well-planned fortifications. But for the first year or two much trouble must probably be expected in this quarter, nor can I well see what measures could be taken to provide against it. The most natural expedient of admitting a foreign protecting force for the first years would be simply suicidal.

The State should be under the control of a European prince, whose religion had better be Protestant, as the Protestants are few and of little importance in Palestine, and there would thus be some guarantee of impartiality in disputes between the two principal Churches. For

nationality an Englishman or a German would
be most suitable, perhaps the former for choice.
Mohammedans have no prejudice against British
rule, and Jews respect England as one of their
most reliable protectors.   On the other hand,
the spread of anti-Semitic ideas in Germany
might make the latter suspicious of German
rulers, with whom also the former have practically no acquaintance.   Nor should it be forgotten that an attempt might easily and innocently
be made to turn the new kingdom of Palestine
here projected into something resembling a German State.   I have not previously spoken of
Germany in connection with the Holy Land,
because, though Germans are likely to be among
the most prominent of its future leaders, it is at
present impossible to foreshadow what part they
may be called upon to play.   The German Government has obtained a footing in Jerusalem by
the cession of the Mouristan, or Hospital of the
Knights of St John.   This is, however, of little
importance, except as indicating a desire on the
part of the Imperial Government not to be quite
left out of the reckoning.   The real importance
of Germany in Palestine comes from the German

Society of the Temple. The original settlers of
this Society had no thoughts but of leaving the
world and addicting themselves to good works,
but the sons who succeed them have no such
all-absorbing ideas of piety. Honest God-fear-
ing men they may be, and I well believe are; but
at the same time they are practical men, full of
enterprise, starting with a knowledge of Palestine
such as few Europeans can ever have, and, at
the same time, with all the prestige acquired
among the natives by the unvarying integrity
and unfailing charity of their fathers. In the
hands of these men the future of Palestine must
lie to a great extent. I do not suspect them of
misusing their power in the least degree, nor do
I even think that they are likely to harbour any
design of putting Palestine into the hands of
Germany, to whom it would be more of a burden
than an advantage. But it is undoubtedly possible that, in a State headed by a German prince,
they might naturally, and perhaps imperceptibly,
create a kind of recognised hegemony of the
German people in Palestine, which, in course of
time, and in less trustworthy hands, might lead
to undesirable results. Therefore I should pre-

fer a prince belonging to the royal family of England, or some other non-German Protestant country, not subject to the influence of France or Russia, whose interests are too deeply at stake to allow of their impartiality. But, indeed, all such questions may well be left for settlement at a time when the first possibility of erecting such a State makes itself manifest.

THE END.

PRINTED BY WILLIAM BLACKWOOD AND SONS.

CATALOGUE

OF

MESSRS BLACKWOOD & SONS'

PUBLICATIONS.

PHILOSOPHICAL CLASSICS FOR ENGLISH READERS.

EDITED BY WILLIAM KNIGHT, LL.D.,
Professor of Moral Philosophy in the University of St Andrews.

In crown 8vo Volumes, with Portraits, price 3s. 6d.

Now ready—

DESCARTES, by Professor Mahaffy, Dublin.—BUTLER, by Rev. W. Lucas Collins, M.A.—BERKELEY, by Professor Campbell Fraser, Edinburgh.—FICHTE, by Professor Adamson, Owens College, Manchester.— KANT, by Professor Wallace, Oxford.— HAMILTON, by Professor Veitch, Glasgow. —HEGEL, by Professor Edward Caird, Glasgow.—LEIBNIZ, by J. Theodore Merz.

—VICO, by Professor Flint, Edinburgh — HOBBES, by Professor Croom Robertson, London.—HUME, by the Editor.—SPINOZA, by the Very Rev. Principal Caird, Glasgow. —BACON: Part I. The Life, by Professor Nichol, Glasgow.—BACON: Part II. Philosophy, by the same Author.—LOCKE, by Professor Campbell Fraser Edinburgh.

In preparation.
MILL, by the Right Hon. A. J. Balfour.

FOREIGN CLASSICS FOR ENGLISH READERS.

EDITED BY MRS OLIPHANT.

In crown 8vo, 2s. 6d.

Contents of the Series.

DANTE, by the Editor.—VOLTAIRE, by General Sir E. B. Hamley, K.C.B. —PASCAL, by Principal Tulloch.—PETRARCH, by Henry Reeve, C.B.—GOETHE, By A. Hayward, Q.C.—MOLIÈRE, by the Editor and F. Tarver, M.A.—MONTAIGNE, by Rev. W. L. Collins, M.A.—RABELAIS, by Walter Besant, M.A.—CALDERON, by E. J. Hasell.—SAINT SIMON, by Clifton W. Collins, M.A.—CERVANTES, by the

Editor. — CORNEILLE AND RACINE, by Henry M. Trollope. — MADAME DE SÉVIGNÉ, by Miss Thackeray.—LA FONTAINE, AND OTHER FRENCH FABULISTS, by Rev. W. Lucas Collins, M.A.—SCHILLER, by James Sime, M.A., Author of 'Lessing, his Life and Writings.'—TASSO, by E. J. Hasell.—ROUSSEAU, by Henry Grey Graham.—ALFRED DE MUSSET, by C. F. Oliphant.

In preparation.
LEOPARDI. By the Editor.

NOW COMPLETE.

ANCIENT CLASSICS FOR ENGLISH READERS.

EDITED BY THE REV. W. LUCAS COLLINS, M.A.

Complete in 28 Vols. crown 8vo, cloth, price 2s. 6d. each. And may also be had in 14 Volumes, strongly and neatly bound, with calf or vellum back, £3, 10s.

Contents of the Series.

HOMER: THE ILIAD, by the Editor.— HOMER: THE ODYSSEY, by the Editor.— HERODOTUS, by George C. Swayne, M.A.— XENOPHON, by Sir Alexander Grant, Bart., LL.D.—EURIPIDES, by W. B. Donne.— ARISTOPHANES, by the Editor.—PLATO, by Clifton W. Collins, M.A.—LUCIAN, by the Editor.—ÆSCHYLUS, by the Right Rev. the Bishop of Colombo.—SOPHOCLES, by Clifton W. Collins, M.A.—HESIOD AND THEOGNIS, by the Rev. J. Davies, M.A.— GREEK ANTHOLOGY, by Lord Neaves.— VIRGIL, by the Editor.—HORACE, by Sir Theodore Martin, K.C.B.—JUVENAL, by Edward Walford, M.A. — PLAUTUS AND

TERENCE, by the Editor.—THE COMMENTARIES OF CÆSAR, by Anthony Trollope. —TACITUS, by W. B. Donne.—CICERO, by the Editor.—PLINY'S LETTERS, by the Rev. Alfred Church, M.A., and the Rev. W J. Brodribb, M.A.—LIVY, by the Editor.—OVID, by the Rev. A. Church, M.A.—CATULLUS, TIBULLUS, AND PROPERTIUS, by the Rev. Jas. Davies, M.A. — DEMOSTHENES, by the Rev. W. J. Brodribb, M.A.—ARISTOTLE, by Sir Alexander Grant, Bart., LL.D.—THUCYDIDES, by the Editor.—LUCRETIUS, by W. H. Mallock, M.A.—PINDAR, by the Rev. F. D. Morice, M.A.

Saturday Review.—"It is difficult to estimate too highly the value of such a series as this in giving 'English readers' an insight, exact as far as it goes, into those olden times which are so remote, and yet to many of us so close."

CATALOGUE

OF

MESSRS BLACKWOOD & SONS'
PUBLICATIONS.

————◆————

ALISON. History of Europe. By Sir ARCHIBALD ALISON, Bart.,
D.C.L.

1. From the Commencement of the French Revolution to the
Battle of Waterloo.
LIBRARY EDITION, 14 vols., with Portraits. Demy 8vo, £10, 10s.
ANOTHER EDITION, in 20 vols. crown 8vo, £6.
PEOPLE'S EDITION, 13 vols. crown 8vo, £2, 11s.

2. Continuation to the Accession of Louis Napoleon.
LIBRARY EDITION, 8 vols. 8vo, £6, 7s. 6d.
PEOPLE'S EDITION, 8 vols. crown 8vo, 34s.

3. Epitome of Alison's History of Europe. Twenty-ninth
Thousand, 7s. 6d.

4. Atlas to Alison's History of Europe. By A. Keith Johnston.
LIBRARY EDITION, demy 4to, £3, 3s.
PEOPLE'S EDITION, 31s. 6d.

—— Life of John Duke of Marlborough. With some Account
of his Contemporaries, and of the War of the Succession. Third Edition.
2 vols. 8vo. Portraits and Maps, 30s.

—— Essays : Historical, Political, and Miscellaneous. 3 vols.
demy 8vo, 45s.

ACTA SANCTORUM HIBERNIÆ ; Ex Codice Salmanticensi.
Nunc primum integre edita opera CAROLI DE SMEDT et JOSEPHI DE BACKER,
e Soc. Jesu, Hagiographorum Bollandianorum ; Auctore et Sumptus Largiente
JOANNE PATRICIO MARCHIONE BOTHAE. In One handsome 4to Volume, bound
in half roxburghe, £2, 2s. ; in paper wrapper, 31s. 6d.

AIRD. Poetical Works of Thomas Aird. Fifth Edition, with
Memoir of the Author by the Rev. JARDINE WALLACE, and Portrait.
Crown 8vo, 7s. 6d.

ALLARDYCE. The City of Sunshine. By ALEXANDER ALLAR-
DYCE. Three vols. post 8vo, £1, 5s. 6d.

—— Memoir of the Honourable George Keith Elphinstone,
K.B., Viscount Keith of Stonehaven, Marischal, Admiral of the Red. 8vo,
with Portrait, Illustrations, and Maps, 21s.

ALMOND. Sermons by a Lay Head-master. By HELY HUTCHIN-
SON ALMOND, M.A. Oxon., Head-master of Loretto School. Crown 8vo, 5s.

ANCIENT CLASSICS FOR ENGLISH READERS. Edited by
Rev. W. LUCAS COLLINS, M.A. Price 2s. 6d. each. *For list of Vols., see page 2.*

AYTOUN. Lays of the Scottish Cavaliers, and other Poems. By
W. EDMONDSTOUNE AYTOUN, D.C.L., Professor of Rhetoric and Belles-Lettres
in the University of Edinburgh. New Edition. Fcap. 8vo, 7s. 6d.
Another Edition, being the Thirtieth. Fcap. 8vo, cloth extra, 7s. 6d.
Cheap Edition. Fcap. 8vo. Illustrated Cover. Price 1s. Cloth, 1s. 3d.

—— An Illustrated Edition of the Lays of the Scottish Cavaliers.
From designs by Sir NOEL PATON. Small 4to, in gilt cloth, 21s.

—— Bothwell : a Poem. Third Edition. Fcap. 7s. 6d.

—— Poems and Ballads of Goethe. Translated by Professor
AYTOUN and Sir THEODORE MARTIN, K.C.B. Third Edition. Fcap., 6s.

AYTOUN. Bon Gaultier's Book of Ballads. By the SAME. Fifteenth
Edition. With Illustrations by Doyle, Leech, and Crowquill Fcap. 8vo, 5s.
———— The Ballads of Scotland. Edited by Professor AYTOUN.
Fourth Edition. 2 vols. fcap. 8vo, 12s.
———— Memoir of William E. Aytoun, D.C.L. By Sir THEODORE
MARTIN, K.C.B. With Portrait. Post 8vo, 12s.
BACH. On Musical Education and Vocal Culture. By ALBERT
B. BACH. Fourth Edition. 8vo, 7s. 6d.
———— The Principles of Singing. A Practical Guide for Vocalists
and Teachers. With Course of Vocal Exercises. Crown 8vo, 6s.
———— The Art of Singing. With Musical Exercises for Young
People. Crown 8vo, 3s.
———— The Art Ballad : Loewe and Schubert. With Music Illus-
trations. With a Portrait of LOEWE Third Edition. Small 4to. 5s.
BALLADS AND POEMS. By MEMBERS OF THE GLASGOW
BALLAD CLUB. Crown 8vo, 7s. 6d
BANNATYNE. Handbook of Republican Institutions in the
United States of America. Based upon Federal and State Laws, and other
reliable sources of information. By DUGALD J. BANNATYNE, Scotch Solicitor,
New York ; Member of the Faculty of Procurators, Glasgow. Cr. 8vo, 7s. 6d.
BELLAIRS. The Transvaal War, 1880-81. Edited by Lady BEL-
LAIRS. With a Frontispiece and Map. 8vo, 15s.
———— Gossips with Girls and Maidens, Betrothed and Free.
New Edition. Crown 8vo, 3s. 6d. Cloth, extra gilt edges, 5s.
BESANT. The Revolt of Man. By WALTER BESANT, M.A.
Ninth Edition. Crown 8vo, 3s. 6d.
———— Readings in Rabelais. Crown 8vo, 7s. 6d.
BEVERIDGE. Culross and Tulliallan; or Perthshire on Forth. Its
History and Antiquities. With Elucidations of Scottish Life and Character
from the Burgh and Kirk-Session Records of that District. By DAVID
BEVERIDGE. 2 vols. 8vo, with Illustrations, 42s.
———— Between the Ochils and the Forth ; or, From Stirling
Bridge to Aberdour. Crown 8vo, 6s.
BLACK. Heligoland and the Islands of the North Sea. By
WILLIAM GEORGE BLACK. Crown 8vo, 4s.
BLACKIE. Lays and Legends of Ancient Greece. By JOHN
STUART BLACKIE, Emeritus Professor of Greek in the University of Edin-
burgh. Second Edition. Fcap. 8vo. 5s.
———— The Wisdom of Goethe. Fcap. 8vo. Cloth, extra gilt, 6s.
———— Scottish Song : Its Wealth, Wisdom, and Social Signifi-
cance. Crown 8vo. With Music. 7s. 6d.
———— A Song of Heroes. Crown 8vo, 6s.
BLACKWOOD'S MAGAZINE, from Commencement in 1817 to
November 1891. Nos. 1 to 913, forming 148 Volumes.
———— Index to Blackwood's Magazine. Vols. 1 to 50. 8vo, 15s.
BLACKWOOD. Tales from Blackwood. Price One Shilling each,
in Paper Cover. Sold separately at all Railway Bookstalls.
They may also be had bound in cloth, 18s., and in half calf, richly gilt, 30s.
Or 12 volumes in 6, roxburghe, 21s., and half red morocco, 28s.
———— Tales from Blackwood. New Series. Complete in Twenty-
four Shilling Parts. Handsomely bound in 12 vols., cloth, 30s. In leather
back, roxburghe style, 37s. 6d. In half calf, gilt, 52s. 6d. In half morocco, 55s.
———— Tales from Blackwood. Third Series. Complete in 6
vols. Handsomely bound in cloth, 15s. ; or in 12 vols. 18s. The 6 vols. bound
in roxburghe, 21s. Half calf, 25s. Half morocco, 28s. Also in 12 parts, price
1s. each.
———— Travel, Adventure, and Sport. From ' Blackwood's
Magazine.' Uniform with ' Tales from Blackwood.' In Twelve Parts, each
price 1s. Or handsomely bound in 6 vols., 15s. Half calf, 25s.

BLACKWOOD. New Uniform Series of Three-and-Sixpenny Novels
(Copyright). Crown 8vo, cloth. Now ready :—

BEGGAR MY NEIGHBOUR. By E. D. Gerard.
THE WATERS OF HERCULES. By the Same.
SONS AND DAUGHTERS. By Mrs Oliphant.
FAIR TO SEE. By L. W. M. Lockhart.
THE REVOLT OF MAN. By Walter Besant.
MINE IS THINE. By L. W. M. Lockhart.
ALTIORA PETO. By Laurence Oliphant.
DOUBLES AND QUITS. By L. W. M. Lockhart.

LADY BABY. By D. Gerard.
HURRISH. By the Hon. Emily Lawless.
THE BLACKSMITH OF VOE. By Paul Cushing.
THE DILEMMA. By the Author of 'The Battle of Dorking.'
MY TRIVIAL LIFE AND MISFORTUNE. By A Plain Woman.
PICCADILLY. By Laurence Oliphant. With Illustrations.

Others in preparation.

—— Standard Novels. Uniform in size and legibly Printed.
Each Novel complete in one volume.

FLORIN SERIES, Illustrated Boards. Or in New Cloth Binding, 2s. 6d.

TOM CRINGLE'S LOG. By Michael Scott.
THE CRUISE OF THE MIDGE. By the Same.
CYRIL THORNTON. By Captain Hamilton.
ANNALS OF THE PARISH. By John Galt.
THE PROVOST, &c. By John Galt.
SIR ANDREW WYLIE. By John Galt.
THE ENTAIL. By John Galt.
MISS MOLLY. By Beatrice May Butt.
REGINALD DALTON. By J. G. Lockhart.

PEN OWEN. By Dean Hook.
ADAM BLAIR. By J. G. Lockhart.
LADY LEE'S WIDOWHOOD. By General Sir E. B. Hamley.
SALEM CHAPEL. By Mrs Oliphant.
THE PERPETUAL CURATE. By Mrs Oliphant.
MISS MARJORIBANKS. By Mrs Oliphant.
JOHN : A Love Story. By Mrs Oliphant.

SHILLING SERIES, Illustrated Cover. Or in New Cloth Binding, 1s. 6d.

THE RECTOR, and THE DOCTOR'S FAMILY. By Mrs Oliphant.
THE LIFE OF MANSIE WAUCH. By D. M. Moir.
PENINSULAR SCENES AND SKETCHES. By F. Hardman.

SIR FRIZZLE PUMPKIN, NIGHTS AT MESS, &c.
THE SUBALTERN.
LIFE IN THE FAR WEST. By G. F. Ruxton.
VALERIUS : A Roman Story. By J. G. Lockhart.

BLACKMORE. The Maid of Sker. By R. D. BLACKMORE, Author of 'Lorna Doone,' &c. New Edition. Crown 8vo, 6s.

BLAIR. History of the Catholic Church of Scotland. From the Introduction of Christianity to the Present Day. By ALPHONS BELLESHEIM, D.D., Canon of Aix-la-Chapelle. Translated, with Notes and Additions, by D. OSWALD HUNTER BLAIR, O.S.B., Monk of Fort Augustus. Complete in 4 vols. demy 8vo, with Maps. Price 12s. 6d. each.

BOSCOBEL TRACTS. Relating to the Escape of Charles the Second after the Battle of Worcester, and his subsequent Adventures. Edited by J. HUGHES, Esq., A.M. A New Edition, with additional Notes and Illustrations, including Communications from the Rev. R. H. BARHAM, Author of the 'Ingoldsby Legends.' 8vo, with Engravings, 16s.

BROUGHAM. Memoirs of the Life and Times of Henry Lord Brougham. Written by HIMSELF. 3 vols. 8vo, £2, 8s. The Volumes are sold separately, price 16s. each.

BROWN. The Forester : A Practical Treatise on the Planting, Rearing, and General Management of Forest-trees. By JAMES BROWN, LL.D., Inspector of and Reporter on Woods and Forests. Fifth Edition, revised and enlarged. Royal 8vo, with Engravings, 36s

BROWN. The Ethics of George Eliot's Works. By JOHN CROMBIE BROWN. Fourth Edition. Crown 8vo, 2s. 6d.

BROWN. A Manual of Botany, Anatomical and Physiological. For the Use of Students. By ROBERT BROWN, M.A., Ph.D. Crown 8vo, with numerous Illustrations, 12s. 6d.

BRUCE. In Clover and Heather. Poems by WALLACE BRUCE. New and Enlarged Edition. Crown 8vo, 4s. 6d.
A limited number of Copies of the First Edition, on large hand-made paper, 12s. 6d.

BRYDALL. Art in Scotland ; its Origin and Progress. By ROBERT BRYDALL, Master of St George's Art School of Glasgow. 8vo, 12s. 6d.

BUCHAN. Introductory Text-Book of Meteorology. By ALEXANDER BUCHAN, M.A., F.R.S.E., Secretary of the Scottish Meteorological Society, &c. Crown 8vo, with 8 Coloured Charts and Engravings, 4s. 6d.

6   LIST OF BOOKS PUBLISHED BY

BUCHANAN. The Shirè Highlands (East Central Africa). By
JOHN BUCHANAN, Planter at Zomba. Crown 8vo, 5s.

BURBIDGE. Domestic Floriculture, Window Gardening, and
Floral Decorations. Being practical directions for the Propagation, Culture,
and Arrangement of Plants and Flowers as Domestic Ornaments. By F. W.
BURBIDGE. Second Edition. Crown 8vo, with numerous Illustrations, 7s. 6d.

—————— Cultivated Plants: Their Propagation and Improvement.
Including Natural and Artificial Hybridisation, Raising from Seed, Cuttings,
and Layers, Grafting and Budding, as applied to the Families and Genera in
Cultivation. Crown 8vo, with numerous Illustrations, 12s. 6d.

BURTON. The History of Scotland : From Agricola's Invasion to
the Extinction of the last Jacobite Insurrection. By JOHN HILL BURTON,
D.C.L., Historiographer-Royal for Scotland. New and Enlarged Edition.
8 vols., and Index. Crown 8vo, £3, 3s.

—————— History of the British Empire during the Reign of Queen
Anne. In 3 vols. 8vo. 36s.

—————— The Scot Abroad. Third Edition. Crown 8vo, 10s. 6d.

—————— The Book-Hunter. New Edition. With Portrait. Crown
8vo, 7s. 6d.

BUTE. The Roman Breviary : Reformed by Order of the Holy
Œcumenical Council of Trent; Published by Order of Pope St Pius V.; and
Revised by Clement VIII. and Urban VIII.; together with the Offices since
granted. Translated out of Latin into English by JOHN, Marquess of Bute,
K.T. In 2 vols, crown 8vo. cloth boards, edges uncut. £2, 2s.

—————— The Altus of St Columba. With a Prose Paraphrase and
Notes. In paper cover, 2s. 6d.

BUTLER. Pompeii : Descriptive and Picturesque. By W.
BUTLER. Post 8vo, 5s.

BUTT. Miss Molly. By BEATRICE MAY BUTT. Cheap Edition, 2s.

—————— Eugenie. Crown 8vo, 6s. 6d.

—————— Elizabeth, and Other Sketches. Crown 8vo, 6s.

—————— Novels. New and Uniform Edition. Crown 8vo, each 2s. 6d.
Delicia. *Now ready.*

CAIRD. Sermons. By JOHN CAIRD, D.D., Principal of the University of Glasgow. Sixteenth Thousand. Fcap. 8vo, 5s.

—————— Religion in Common Life. A Sermon preached in Crathie
Church, October 14, 1855, before Her Majesty the Queen and Prince Albert.
Published by Her Majesty's Command. Cheap Edition, 3d.

CAMPBELL. Critical Studies in St Luke's Gospel : Its Demonology
and Ebionitism. By COLIN CAMPBELL, B.D., Minister of the Parish of Dun-
dee, formerly Scholar and Fellow of Glasgow University. Author of the 'Three
First Gospels in Greek, arranged in parallel columns. Post 8vo, 7s. 6d.

CAMPBELL. Sermons Preached before the Queen at Balmoral.
By the Rev. A. A. CAMPBELL, Minister of Crathie. Published by Command
of Her Majesty. Crown 8vo, 4s. 6d.

CAMPBELL. Records of Argyll. Legends, Traditions, and Recollections of Argyllshire Highlanders, collected chiefly from the Gaelic.
With Notes on the Antiquity of the Dress, Clan Colours or Tartans of the
Highlanders. By LORD ARCHIBALD CAMPBELL. Illustrated with Nineteen
full-page Etchings. 4to, printed on hand-made paper, £3, 3s.

CANTON. A Lost Epic, and other Poems. By WILLIAM CANTON.
Crown 8vo, 5s.

CARRICK. Koumiss ; or, Fermented Mare's Milk : and its Uses
in the Treatment and Cure of Pulmonary Consumption, and other Wasting
Diseases. With an Appendix on the best Methods of Fermenting Cow's Milk.
By GEORGE L. CARRICK, M.D., L.R.C.S.E. and L.R.C.P.E., Physician to the
British Embassy, St Petersburg, &c. Crown 8vo, 10s. 6d.

CARSTAIRS. British Work in India. By R. CARSTAIRS. Cr. 8vo, 6s.

CAUVIN. A Treasury of the English and German Languages.
Compiled from the best Authors and Lexicographers in both Languages.
By JOSEPH CAUVIN, LL.D. and Ph.D., of the University of Göttingen, &c.
Crown 8vo, 7s. 6d.

CAVE-BROWN. Lambeth Palace and its Associations. By J.
CAVE-BROWN, M.A., Vicar of Detling, Kent, and for many years Curate of Lambeth Parish Church. With an Introduction by the Archbishop of Canterbury.
Second Edition, containing an additional Chapter on Medieval Life in the
Old Palaces. 8vo, with Illustrations, 21s.

CHARTERIS. Canonicity; or, Early Testimonies to the Existence
and Use of the Books of the New Testament. Based on Kirchhoffer's 'Quellensammlung.' Edited by A. H. CHARTERIS, D.D., Professor of Biblical
Criticism in the University of Edinburgh. 8vo, 18s.

CHRISTISON. Life of Sir Robert Christison, Bart., M.D., D.C.L.
Oxon., Professor of Medical Jurisprudence in the University of Edinburgh.
Edited by his SONS. In two vols. 8vo. Vol. I.—Autobiography. 16s. Vol. II.
—Memoirs. 16s.

CHURCH SERVICE SOCIETY. A Book of Common Order :
Being Forms of Worship issued by the Church Service Society. Sixth Edition. Crown, 8vo, 6s. Also in 2 vols, crown 8vo, 6s. 6d.

CLELAND. Too Apt a Pupil. By ROBERT CLELAND. Author
of 'Barbara Allan, the Provost's Daughter.' Crown 8vo, 6s.

CLOUSTON. Popular Tales and Fictions: their Migrations and
Transformations. By W. A. CLOUSTON, Editor of 'Arabian Poetry for English Readers,' &c. 2 vols. post 8vo, roxburghe binding, 25s.

COBBAN. Master of his Fate. By J. MACLAREN COBBAN, Author
of 'The Cure of Souls,' 'Tinted Vapours,' &c. New and Cheaper Edition.
Crown 8vo, paper cover, 1s. Cloth, bevelled boards, 3s. 6d.

COCHRAN. A Handy Text-Book of Military Law. Compiled
chiefly to assist Officers preparing for Examination; also for all Officers of
the Regular and Auxiliary Forces. Comprising also a Synopsis of part of
the Army Act. By Major F. COCHRAN, Hampshire Regiment Garrison Instructor, North British District. Crown 8vo, 7s. 6d.

COLQUHOUN. The Moor and the Loch. Containing Minute
Instructions in all Highland Sports, with Wanderings over Crag and Corrie,
Flood and Fell. By JOHN COLQUHOUN. Seventh Edition. With Illustrations. 8vo, 21s.

COTTERILL. Suggested Reforms in Public Schools. By C. C.
COTTERILL, M.A. Crown 8vo, 3s. 6d.

CRANSTOUN. The Elegies of Albius Tibullus. Translated into
English Verse, with Life of the Poet, and Illustrative Notes. By JAMES CRANSTOUN, LL.D., Author of a Translation of 'Catullus.' Crown 8vo, 6s. 6d.

—— The Elegies of Sextus Propertius. Translated into English
Verse, with Life of the Poet, and Illustrative Notes. Crown 8vo, 7s. 6d.

CRAWFORD. Saracinesca. By F. MARION CRAWFORD, Author of
'Mr Isaacs,' 'Dr Claudius,' 'Zoroaster,' &c. &c. Fifth Ed. Crown 8vo, 6s.

CRAWFORD. The Doctrine of Holy Scripture respecting the
Atonement. By the late THOMAS J. CRAWFORD, D.D., Professor of Divinity in
the University of Edinburgh. Fifth Edition. 8vo, 12s.

—— The Fatherhood of God, Considered in its General
and Special Aspects. Third Edition, Revised and Enlarged. 8vo, 9s.

—— The Preaching of the Cross, and other Sermons. 8vo, 7s. 6d.

—— The Mysteries of Christianity. Crown 8vo, 7s. 6d.

CRAWFORD. An Atonement of East London, and other Poems.
By HOWARD CRAWFORD, M.A. Crown 8vo, 5s.

CUSHING. The Blacksmith of Voe. By PAUL CUSHING, Author
of 'The Bull i' th' Thorn.' Cheap Edition. Crown 8vo, 3s. 6d.

—— Cut with his own Diamond. A Novel. 3 vols. cr. 8vo, 25s. 6d.

DAVIES. Norfolk Broads and Rivers ; or, The Waterways, Lagoons, and Decoys of East Anglia. By G. CHRISTOPHER DAVIES. Illustrated with Seven full-page Plates. New and Cheaper Edition. Crown 8vo, 6s.

——— Our Home in Aveyron. Sketches of Peasant Life in Aveyron and the Lot. By G. CHRISTOPHER DAVIES and Mrs BROUGHALL. Illustrated with full-page Illustrations. 8vo, 15s. Cheap Edition, 7s. 6d.

DAYNE. In the Name of the Tzar. A Novel. By J. BELFORD DAYNE. Crown 8vo, 6s.

——— Tribute to Satan. A Novel. Crown 8vo, 2s. 6d.

DE LA WARR. An Eastern Cruise in the 'Edeline.' By the Countess DE LA WARR. In Illustrated Cover. 2s.

DESCARTES. The Method, Meditations, and Principles of Philosophy of Descartes. Translated from the Original French and Latin. With a New Introductory Essay, Historical and Critical, on the Cartesian Philosophy. By Professor VEITCH, LL.D., Glasgow University. Ninth Edition. 6s. 6d.

DICKSON. Gleanings from Japan. By W. G. DICKSON, Author of 'Japan : Being a Sketch of its History, Government, and Officers of the Empire.' With Illustrations. 8vo, 16s.

DOGS, OUR DOMESTICATED : Their Treatment in reference to Food, Diseases, Habits, Punishment, Accomplishments. By 'MAGENTA.' Crown 8vo, 2s. 6d.

DOMESTIC EXPERIMENT, A. By the Author of 'Ideala : A Study from Life.' Crown 8vo, 6s.

DR HERMIONE. By the Author of 'Lady Bluebeard,' 'Zit and Xoe.' Crown 8vo, 6s.

DU CANE. The Odyssey of Homer, Books I.-XII. Translated into English Verse. By Sir CHARLES DU CANE, K.C.M.G. 8vo, 10s. 6d.

DUDGEON. History of the Edinburgh or Queen's Regiment · Light Infantry Militia, now 3rd Battalion The Royal Scots ; with an Account of the Origin and Progress of the Militia, and a Brief Sketch of the old Royal Scots. By Major R. C. DUDGEON, Adjutant 3rd Battalion The Royal Scots. Post 8vo, with Illustrations, 10s. 6d.

DUNCAN. Manual of the General Acts of Parliament relating to the Salmon Fisheries of Scotland from 1828 to 1882. By J. BARKER DUNCAN. Crown 8vo, 5s.

DUNSMORE. Manual of the Law of Scotland as to the Relations between Agricultural Tenants and their Landlords, Servants, Merchants, and Bowers. By W. DUNSMORE. 8vo, 7s. 6d.

DUPRÉ. Thoughts on Art, and Autobiographical Memoirs of Giovanni Duprè. Translated from the Italian by E. M. PERUZZI, with the permission of the Author. New Edition. With an Introduction by W. W. STORY. Crown 8vo, 10s. 6d.

ELIOT. George Eliot's Life, Related in her Letters and Journals. Arranged and Edited by her husband, J. W. CROSS. With Portrait and other Illustrations. Third Edition. 3 vols. post 8vo, 42s.

——— George Eliot's Life. (Cabinet Edition.) With Portrait and other Illustrations. 3 vols. crown 8vo, 15s.

——— George Eliot's Life. With Portrait and other Illustrations. New Edition, in one volume. Crown 8vo, 7s. 6d.

——— Works of George Eliot (Cabinet Edition). Handsomely printed in a new type, 21 volumes, crown 8vo, price £5, 5s. The Volumes are also sold separately, price 5s. each, viz. :—
Romola. 2 vols.—Silas Marner, The Lifted Veil, Brother Jacob. 1 vol.—Adam Bede. 2 vols.—Scenes of Clerical Life. 2 vols.—The Mill on the Floss. 2 vols.—Felix Holt. 2 vols.—Middlemarch. 3 vols.—Daniel Deronda. 3 vols.—The Spanish Gypsy. 1 vol.—Jubal, and other Poems, Old and New. 1 vol.—Theophrastus Such. 1 vol.—Essays. 1 vol.

——— Novels by GEORGE ELIOT. Cheap Edition. Adam Bede. Illustrated. 3s. 6d., cloth.—The Mill on the Floss. Illustrated. 3s. 6d., cloth.—Scenes of Clerical Life. Illustrated. 3s., cloth.—Silas Marner : the Weaver of Raveloe. Illustrated. 2s. 6d., cloth.—Felix Holt, the Radical. Illustrated. 3s. 6d., cloth.—Romola. With Vignette. 3s. 6d., cloth.

ELIOT. Middlemarch. Crown 8vo, 7s. 6d.
—— Daniel Deronda. Crown 8vo, 7s. 6d.
—— Essays. New Edition. Crown 8vo, 5s.
—— Impressions of Theophrastus Such. New Ed. Cr. 8vo, 5s.
—— The Spanish Gypsy. New Edition. Crown 8vo, 5s.
—— The Legend of Jubal, and other Poems, Old and New.
New Edition. Crown 8vo, 5s.
—— Wise, Witty, and Tender Sayings, in Prose and Verse.
Selected from the Works of GEORGE ELIOT. Eighth Edition. Fcap. 8vo, 6s.
—— The George Eliot Birthday Book. Printed on fine paper,
with red border, and handsomely bound in cloth, gilt. Fcap. 8vo, cloth, 3s. 6d.
And in French morocco or Russia, 5s.
ESSAYS ON SOCIAL SUBJECTS. Originally published in the
'Saturday Review.' New Ed. First & Second Series. 2 vols. cr. 8vo, 6s. each.
EWALD. The Crown and its Advisers ; or, Queen, Ministers,
Lords and Commons. By ALEXANDER CHARLES EWALD, F.S.A. Crown 8vo, 5s.
FAITHS OF THE WORLD, The. A Concise History of the
Great Religious Systems of the World. By various Authors. Crown 8vo, 5s.
FARRER. A Tour in Greece in 1880. By RICHARD RIDLEY
FARRER. With Twenty-seven full-page Illustrations by LORD WINDSOR.
Royal 8vo, with a Map, 21s.
FERRIER. Philosophical Works of the late James F. Ferrier,
B.A. Oxon., Professor of Moral Philosophy and Political Economy, St Andrews.
New Edition. Edited by Sir ALEX. GRANT, Bart., D.C.L., and Professor
LUSHINGTON. 3 vols. crown 8vo, 34s. 6d.
—— Institutes of Metaphysic. Third Edition. 10s. 6d.
—— Lectures on the Early Greek Philosophy. 3d Ed. 10s. 6d.
—— Philosophical Remains, including the Lectures on Early
Greek Philosophy. 2 vols., 24s.
FITZROY. Dogma and the Church of England. By A. I. FITZROY.
Post 8vo, 7s. 6d.
FLINT. The Philosophy of History in Europe. By ROBERT
FLINT, D.D., LL.D., Professor of Divinity, University of Edinburgh. 2 vols.
8vo. [New Edition in preparation.
—— Theism. Being the Baird Lecture for 1876. Seventh Edi-
tion. Crown 8vo, 7s. 6d.
—— Anti-Theistic Theories. Being the Baird Lecture for 1877.
Fourth Edition. Crown 8vo, 10s. 6d.
—— Agnosticism. Being the Croall Lectures for 1887-88.
[In the press.
FORBES. Insulinde: Experiences of a Naturalist's Wife in the
Eastern Archipelago. By Mrs H. O. FORBES. Crown 8vo, with a Map. 4s. 6d.
FOREIGN CLASSICS FOR ENGLISH READERS. Edited
by Mrs OLIPHANT. Price 2s. 6d. For List of Volumes published, see page 2.
FOSTER. The Fallen City, and Other Poems. By WILL FOSTER.
In 1 vol. Crown 8vo. [Immediately.
FULLARTON. Merlin: A Dramatic Poem. By RALPH MACLEOD
FULLARTON. Crown 8vo, 5s.
GALT. Novels by JOHN GALT. Fcap. 8vo, boards, 2s.; cloth, 2s. 6d.
Annals of the Parish.—The Provost.—Sir Andrew Wylie.—
The Entail.
GENERAL ASSEMBLY OF THE CHURCH OF SCOTLAND.
—— Prayers for Social and Family Worship. Prepared by a
Special Committee of the General Assembly of the Church of Scotland. En-
tirely New Edition, Revised and Enlarged. Fcap. 8vo, red edges, 2s.
—— Prayers for Family Worship. A Selection from the com-
plete book. Fcap. 8vo, red edges, price 1s.

GENERAL ASSEMBLY OF THE CHURCH OF SCOTLAND.
—— Scottish Hymnal, with Appendix Incorporated. Published for Use in Churches by Authority of the General Assembly. 1. Large type, cloth, red edges, 2s. 6d. ; French morocco, 4s. 2. Bourgeois type, limp cloth, 1s.; French morocco, 2s. 3. Nonpareil type, cloth, red edges, 6d. ; French morocco, 1s. 4d. 4. Paper covers, 3d. 5. Sunday-School Edition, paper covers, 1d. No. 1, bound with the Psalms and Paraphrases, French morocco, 8s. No. 2, bound with the Psalms and Paraphrases, cloth, 2s. ; French morocco, 3s.

GERARD. Reata: What's in a Name. By E. D. GERARD. New Edition. Crown 8vo, 6s.

—— Beggar my Neighbour. Cheap Edition. Crown 8vo, 3s. 6d.

—— The Waters of Hercules. Cheap Edition. Crown 8vo, 3s. 6d.

GERARD. The Land beyond the Forest. Facts, Figures, and Fancies from Transylvania. By E. GERARD. In Two Volumes. With Maps and Illustrations. 25s.

—— Bis : Some Tales Retold. Crown 8vo, 6s.

—— A Secret Mission. 2 vols. crown 8vo, 17s.

GERARD. Lady Baby. By DOROTHEA GERARD, Author of 'Orthodox.' Cheap Edition. Crown 8vo, 3s. 6d.

—— Recha. Second Edition. Crown 8vo, 6s.

GERARD. Stonyhurst Latin Grammar. By Rev. JOHN GERARD. Fcap. 8vo, 3s.

GILL. Free Trade : an Inquiry into the Nature of its Operation. By RICHARD GILL. Crown 8vo, 7s. 6d.

—— Free Trade under Protection. Crown 8vo, 7s. 6d.

GOETHE'S FAUST. Translated into English Verse by Sir THEODORE MARTIN, K.C.B. Part I. Second Edition, post 8vo, 6s. Ninth Edition, fcap., 3s. 6d. Part II. Second Edition, revised. Fcap. 8vo, 6s.

GOETHE. Poems and Ballads of Goethe. Translated by Professor AYTOUN and Sir THEODORE MARTIN, K.C.B. Third Edition, fcap. 8vo, 6s.

GOODALL. Juxta Crucem. Studies of the Love that is over us. By the late Rev. CHARLES GOODALL, B.D., Minister of Barr. With a Memoir by Rev. Dr Strong, Glasgow, and Portrait. Crown 8vo, 6s.

GORDON CUMMING. Two Happy Years in Ceylon. By C. F. GORDON CUMMING. With 15 full-page Illustrations and a Map. 2 vols. 8vo, 30s.

—— At Home in Fiji. Fourth Edition, post 8vo. With Illustrations and Map. 7s. 6d.

—— A Lady's Cruise in a French Man-of-War. New and Cheaper Edition. 8vo. With Illustrations and Map. 12s. 6d.

—— Fire-Fountains. The Kingdom of Hawaii: Its Volcanoes, and the History of its Missions. With Map and Illustrations. 2 vols. 8vo, 25s.

—— Wanderings in China. New and Cheaper Edition. 8vo, with Illustrations, 10s.

—— Granite Crags: The Yō-semité Region of California. Illustrated with 8 Engravings. New and Cheaper Edition. 8vo, 8s. 6d

GRAHAM. The Life and Work of Syed Ahmed Khan, C.S.I. By Lieut.-Colonel G. F. I. GRAHAM, B.S.C. 8vo, 14s.

GRAHAM. Manual of the Elections (Scot.) (Corrupt and Illegal Practices) Act, 1890. With Analysis, Relative Act of Sederunt, Appendix containing the Corrupt Practices Acts of 1883 and 1885, and Copious Index. By J. EDWARD GRAHAM, Advocate. 8vo, 4s. 6d.

GRANT. Bush-Life in Queensland. By A. C. GRANT. New Edition. Crown 8vo, 6s.

GRIFFITHS. Locked Up. By Major ARTHUR GRIFFITHS, Author of 'The Wrong Road,' 'Chronicles of Newgate,' &c. With Illustrations by C. J. STANILAND, R.I. Crown 8vo, 2s. 6d.

GUTHRIE-SMITH. Crispus : A Drama. By H. GUTHRIE-SMITH. In one volume. Fcap. 4to, 5s.

HAINES. Unless! A Romance. By RANDOLPH HAINES. Crown 8vo, 6s.

HALDANE. Subtropical Cultivations and Climates. A Handy Book for Planters, Colonists, and Settlers. By R. C. HALDANE. Post 8vo, 9s.

HALLETT. A Thousand Miles on an Elephant in the Shan States. By HOLT S. HALLETT, M. Inst. C.E., F.R.G.S., M.R.A.S., Hon. Member Manchester and Tyneside Geographical Societies. 8vo, with Maps and numerous Illustrations, 21s.

HAMERTON. Wenderholme : A Story of Lancashire and Yorkshire Life. By PHILIP GILBERT HAMERTON, Author of 'A Painter's Camp.' A New Edition. Crown 8vo, 6s.

HAMILTON. Lectures on Metaphysics. By Sir WILLIAM HAMILTON, Bart., Professor of Logic and Metaphysics in the University of Edinburgh. Edited by the Rev. H. L. MANSEL, B.D., LL.D., Dean of St Paul's ; and JOHN VEITCH, M.A., LL.D., Professor of Logic and Rhetoric, Glasgow. Seventh Edition. 2 vols. 8vo, 24s.

———— Lectures on Logic. Edited by the SAME. Third Edition. 2 vols., 24s.

———— Discussions on Philosophy and Literature, Education and University Reform. Third Edition, 8vo, 21s.

———— Memoir of Sir William Hamilton, Bart., Professor of Logic and Metaphysics in the University of Edinburgh. By Professor VEITCH, of the University of Glasgow. 8vo, with Portrait, 18s.

———— Sir William Hamilton : The Man and his Philosophy. Two Lectures delivered before the Edinburgh Philosophical Institution, January and February 1883. By the SAME. Crown 8vo, 2s.

HAMLEY. The Operations of War Explained and Illustrated. By General Sir EDWARD BRUCE HAMLEY, K.C.B., K.C.M.G., M.P. Fifth Edition, revised throughout. 4to, with numerous Illustrations, 30s.

———— National Defence ; Articles and Speeches. Post 8vo, 6s.

———— Shakespeare's Funeral, and other Papers. Post 8vo, 7s. 6d.

———— Thomas Carlyle : An Essay. Second Ed. Cr. 8vo, 2s. 6d.

———— On Outposts. Second Edition. 8vo, 2s.

———— Wellington's Career ; A Military and Political Summary. Crown 8vo, 2s.

———— Lady Lee's Widowhood. Crown 8vo, 2s. 6d.

———— Our Poor Relations. A Philozoic Essay. With Illustrations, chiefly by Ernest Griset Crown 8vo, cloth gilt, 3s. 6d.

HAMLEY. Guilty, or Not Guilty ? A Tale. By Major-General W. G. HAMLEY, late of the Royal Engineers. New Edition. Crown 8vo, 3s. 6d.

HARRISON. The Scot in Ulster. The Story of the Scottish Settlement in Ulster. By JOHN HARRISON, Author of ' Oure Tounis Colledge.' Crown 8vo, 2s. 6d.

HASELL. Bible Partings. By E. J. HASELL. Crown 8vo, 6s.

———— Short Family Prayers. Cloth, 1s.

HAY. The Works of the Right Rev. Dr George Hay, Bishop of Edinburgh. Edited under the Supervision of the Right Rev. Bishop STRAIN. With Memoir and Portrait of the Author. 5 vols. crown 8vo, bound in extra cloth, £1, 1s. The following Volumes may be had separately—viz. : The Devout Christian Instructed in the Law of Christ from the Written Word. 2 vols., 8s.—The Pious Christian Instructed in the Nature and Practice of the Principal Exercises of Piety. 1 vol.. 3s.

HEATLEY. The Horse-Owner's Safeguard. A Handy Medical Guide for every Man who owns a Horse. By G. S. HEATLEY, M.R.C.V.S. Crown 8vo, 5s.

———— The Stock-Owner's Guide. A Handy Medical Treatise for every Man who owns an Ox or a Cow. Crown 8vo, 4s. 6d.

HEDDERWICK. Lays of Middle Age ; and other Poems. By JAMES HEDDERWICK, LL.D. Price 3s. 6d.

HEDDERWICK. Backward Glances; or, Some Personal Recollections. With a Portrait. Post 8vo, 7s. 6d.

HEMANS. The Poetical Works of Mrs Hemans. Copyright Edi-
tions.—Royal 8vo, 5s.—The Same, with Engravings, cloth, gilt edges, 7s. 6d.
—Six Vols. in Three, fcap., 12s. 6d.
SELECT POEMS OF MRS HEMANS. Fcap., cloth, gilt edges, 3s.

HERKLESS. Cardinal Beaton Priest and Politician. By JOHN
HERKLESS, Minister of Tannadice. With a Portrait. Post 8vo, 7s. 6d.

HOME PRAYERS. By Ministers of the Church of Scotland and
Members of the Church Service Society. Second Edition. Fcap. 8vo, 3s.

HOMER. The Odyssey. Translated into English Verse in the
Spenserian Stanza. By PHILIP STANHOPE WORSLEY. Third Edition, 2 vols.
fcap., 12s.

————— The Iliad. Translated by P. S. WORSLEY and Professor
CONINGTON. 2 vols. crown 8vo, 21s.

HUTCHINSON. Hints on the Game of Golf. By HORACE G.
HUTCHINSON. Sixth Edition, Enlarged. Fcap. 8vo, cloth, 1s.

IDDESLEIGH. Lectures and Essays. By the late EARL OF
IDDESLEIGH, G.C.B., D.C.L., &c. 8vo, 16s.

————— Life, Letters, and Diaries of Sir Stafford Northcote, First
Earl of Iddesleigh. By ANDREW LANG. With Three Portraits and a View of
Pynes. Third Edition. 2 vols. Post 8vo, 31s. 6d.
POPULAR EDITION. In one volume. With two Engravings. Post 8vo, 7s. 6d.

INDEX GEOGRAPHICUS : Being a List, alphabetically arranged,
of the Principal Places on the Globe, with the Countries and Subdivisions of
the Countries in which they are situated, and their Latitudes and Longitudes.
Imperial 8vo, pp. 676, 21s.

JEAN JAMBON. Our Trip to Blunderland ; or, Grand Excursion
to Blundertown and Back. By JEAN JAMBON. With Sixty Illustrations
designed by CHARLES DOYLE, engraved by DALZIEL. Fourth Thousand.
Cloth, gilt edges, 6s. 6d. Cheap Edition, cloth, 3s. 6d. Boards, 2s. 6d.

JENNINGS. Mr Gladstone : A Study. By LOUIS J. JENNINGS,
M.P., Author of 'Republican Government in the United States,' 'The Croker
Memoirs,' &c. Popular Edition. Crown 8vo, 1s.

JERNINGHAM. Reminiscences of an Attaché. By HUBERT
E. H. JERNINGHAM. Second Edition. Crown 8vo, 5s.

————— Diane de Breteuille. A Love Story. Crown 8vo, 2s. 6d.

JOHNSTON. The Chemistry of Common Life. By Professor
J. F. W. JOHNSTON. New Edition, Revised, and brought down to date. By
ARTHUR HERBERT CHURCH, M.A. Oxon.; Author of 'Food: its Sources,
Constituents, and Uses,' &c. With Maps and 102 Engravings. Cr. 8vo, 7s. 6d.

————— Elements of Agricultural Chemistry and Geology. Revised, and brought down to date. By Sir CHARLES A. CAMERON, M.D.,
F.R.C.S.I., &c. Sixteenth Edition. Fcap. 8vo, 6s. 6d.

————— Catechism of Agricultural Chemistry and Geology. New
Edition, revised and enlarged, by Sir C. A. CAMERON. Eighty-sixth Thousand, with numerous Illustrations, 1s.

JOHNSTON. Patrick Hamilton : a Tragedy of the Reformation
in Scotland, 1528. By T. P. JOHNSTON. Crown 8vo, with Two Etchings. 5s.

KER. Short Studies on St Paul's Letter to the Philippians. By
Rev. WILLIAM LEE KER, Minister of Kilwinning. Crown 8vo, 5s.

KING. The Metamorphoses of Ovid. Translated in English Blank
Verse. By HENRY KING, M.A., Fellow of Wadham College, Oxford, and of
the Inner Temple, Barrister-at-Law. Crown 8vo, 10s. 6d.

KINGLAKE. History of the Invasion of the Crimea. By A. W.
KINGLAKE. Cabinet Edition. revised. With an Index to the Complete Work.
Illustrated with Maps and Plans. Complete in 9 Vols., crown 8vo, at 6s. each.

KINGLAKE. History of the Invasion of the Crimea. Demy 8vo. Vol. VI. Winter Troubles. With a Map, 16s. Vols. VII. and VIII. From the Morrow of Inkerman to the Death of Lord Raglan. With an Index to the Whole Work. With Maps and Plans. 28s.

―――― Eothen. A New Edition, uniform with the Cabinet Edition of the 'History of the Invasion of the Crimea,' price 6s.

KNEIPP. My Water-Cure. As Tested through more than Thirty Years, and Described for the Healing of Diseases and the Preservation of Health. By SEBASTIAN KNEIPP, Parish Priest of Wörishofen (Bavaria). With a Portrait and other Illustrations. Only Authorised English Translation. Translated from the Thirtieth German Edition by A. de F. Crown 8vo, 5s.

KNOLLYS. The Elements of Field-Artillery. Designed for the Use of Infantry and Cavalry Officers. By HENRY KNOLLYS, Captain Royal Artillery; Author of 'From Sedan to Saarbrück,' Editor of 'Incidents in the Sepoy War,' &c. With Engravings. Crown 8vo, 7s. 6d.

LAMINGTON. In the Days of the Dandies. By the late Lord LAMINGTON. Crown 8vo. Illustrated cover, 1s.; cloth, 1s. 6d.

LAWLESS. Hurrish : a Study. By the Hon. EMILY LAWLESS, Author of 'A Chelsea Householder,' &c. Fourth Edition, crown 8vo, 3s. 6d.

LAWSON. Spain of To-day : A Descriptive, Industrial, and Financial Survey of the Peninsula, with a full account of the Rio Tinto Mines. By W. R. LAWSON. Crown 8vo, 3s 6d.

LEES. A Handbook of Sheriff Court Styles. By J. M. LEES, M.A., LL.B., Advocate, Sheriff-Substitute of Lanarkshire. New Ed., 8vo, 21s.

―――― A Handbook of the Sheriff and Justice of Peace Small Debt Courts. 8vo, 7s. 6d.

LIGHTFOOT. Studies in Philosophy. By the Rev. J. LIGHTFOOT, M.A., D.Sc., Vicar of Cross Stone, Todmorden. Crown 8vo, 4s. 6d.

LOCKHART. Novels by LAURENCE W. M. LOCKHART. See Blackwoods' New Series of Three-and-Sixpenny Novels on page 5.

LORIMER. The Institutes of Law : A Treatise of the Principles of Jurisprudence as determined by Nature. By the late JAMES LORIMER, Professor of Public Law and of the Law of Nature and Nations in the University of Edinburgh. New Edition, revised and much enlarged. 8vo, 18s.

―――― The Institutes of the Law of Nations. A Treatise of the Jural Relation of Separate Political Communities. In 2 vols. 8vo. Volume I., price 16s. Volume II., price 20s.

LOVE. Scottish Church Music. Its Composers and Sources. With Musical Illustrations. By JAMES LOVE. In 1 vol. post 8vo, 7s. 6d.

M'COMBIE. Cattle and Cattle-Breeders. By WILLIAM M'COMBIE, Tillyfour. New Edition, enlarged, with Memoir of the Author. By JAMES MACDONALD, of the 'Farming World.' Crown 8vo, 3s. 6d.

MACRAE. A Handbook of Deer-Stalking. By ALEXANDER MACRAE, late Forester to Lord Henry Bentinck. With Introduction by HORATIO ROSS, Esq. Fcap. 8vo, with two Photographs from Life. 3s. 6d.

M'CRIE. Works of the Rev. Thomas M'Crie, D.D. Uniform Edition. Four vols. crown 8vo, 24s.

―――― Life of John Knox. Containing Illustrations of the History of the Reformation in Scotland. Crown 8vo. 6s. Another Edition, 3s. 6d.

―――― Life of Andrew Melville. Containing Illustrations of the Ecclesiastical and Literary History of Scotland in the Sixteenth and Seventeenth Centuries. Crown 8vo, 6s.

―――― History of the Progress and Suppression of the Reformation in Italy in the Sixteenth Century. Crown 8vo, 4s.

―――― History of the Progress and Suppression of the Reformation in Spain in the Sixteenth Century. Crown 8vo, 3s. 6d.

―――― Lectures on the Book of Esther. Fcap. 8vo, 5s.

MACDONALD. A Manual of the Criminal Law (Scotland) Procedure Act, 1887. By NORMAN DORAN MACDONALD. Revised by the LORD JUSTICE-CLERK. 8vo, cloth, 10s. 6d.

MACGREGOR. Life and Opinions of Major-General Sir Charles MacGregor, K.C.B., C.S.I., C.I.E , Quartermaster-General of India. From his Letters and Diaries. Edited by LADY MACGREGOR. With Portraits and Maps to illustrate Campaigns in which he was engaged. 2 vols. 8vo, 35s.

M'INTOSH. The Book of the Garden. By CHARLES M'INTOSH, formerly Curator of the Royal Gardens of his Majesty the King of the Belgians, and lately of those of his Grace the Duke of Buccleuch, K.G., at Dalkeith Palace. 2 vols. royal 8vo, with 1350 Engravings. £4, 7s. 6d. Vol. I. On the Formation of Gardens and Construction of Garden Edifices. £2, 10s. Vol. II. Practical Gardening. £1, 17s. 6d.

MACINTYRE. Hindu-Koh : Wanderings and Wild Sports on and beyond the Himalayas. By Major-General DONALD MACINTYRE, V.C., late Prince of Wales' Own Goorkhas, F.R.G.S. *Dedicated to H.R.H. The Prince of Wales.* New and Cheaper Edition, revised, with numerous Illustrations, post 8vo, 7s. 6d.

MACKAY. A Sketch of the History of Fife and Kinross. A Study of Scottish History and Character. By Æ. J. G. MACKAY, Sheriff of these Counties. Crown 8vo, 6s.

MACKAY. A Manual of Modern Geography ; Mathematical, Physical, and Political. By the Rev. ALEXANDER MACKAY, LL.D., F.R.G.S. 11th Thousand, revised to the present time. Crown 8vo, pp. 688. 7s. 6d.

—— Elements of Modern Geography. 53d Thousand, revised to the present time. Crown 8vo, pp. 300, 3s.

—— The Intermediate Geography. Intended as an Intermediate Book between the Author's 'Outlines of Geography' and ' Elements of Geography.' Fifteenth Edition, revised. Crown 8vo, pp. 238, 2s.

—— Outlines of Modern Geography. 188th Thousand, revised to the present time. 18mo, pp. 118, 1s.

—— First Steps in Geography. 105th Thousand. 18mo, pp. 56. Sewed, 4d. ; cloth, 6d.

—— Elements of Physiography and Physical Geography. With Express Reference to the Instructions issued by the Science and Art Department. 30th Thousand, revised. Crown 8vo, 1s. 6d.

—— Facts and Dates ; or, the Leading Events in Sacred and Profane History, and the Principal Facts in the various Physical Sciences. For Schools and Private Reference. New Edition. Crown 8vo, 3s. 6d.

MACKAY. An Old Scots Brigade. Being the History of Mackay's Regiment, now incorporated with the Royal Scots. With an Appendix containing many Original Documents connected with the History of the Regiment. By JOHN MACKAY (late) OF HERRIESDALE. Crown 8vo, 5s.

MACKENZIE. Studies in Roman Law. With Comparative Views of the Laws of France, England, and Scotland. By LORD MACKENZIE, one of the Judges of the Court of Session in Scotland. Sixth Edition, Edited by JOHN KIRKPATRICK, Esq., M.A., LL.B., Advocate, Professor of History in the University of Edinburgh. 8vo, 12s.

M'KERLIE. Galloway : Ancient and Modern. An Account of the Historic Celtic District. By P. H. M'KERLIE, F.S.A. Scot., F.R.G.S., &c. Author of 'Lands and their Owners in Galloway.' Crown 8vo, 7s. 6d.

M'PHERSON. Summer Sundays in a Strathmore Parish. By J. GORDON M'PHERSON, Ph.D., F.R.S.E., Minister of Ruthven. Crown 8vo, 5s.

—— Golf and Golfers. Past and Present. With an Introduction by the Right Hon. A. J. BALFOUR, and a Portrait of the Author. Fcap. 8vo, 1s. 6d.

MARSHALL. It Happened Yesterday. A Novel. Crown 8vo, 6s.

MARSHMAN. History of India. From the Earliest Period to the Close of the India Company's Government; with an Epitome of Subsequent Events. By JOHN CLARK MARSHMAN, C.S.I. Abridged from the Author's larger work. Second Edition, revised. Crown 8vo, with Map, 6s. 6d.

MARTIN. Goethe's Faust. Part I. Translated by Sir THEODORE MARTIN, K.C.B. Second Ed., crown 8vo, 6s. Ninth Ed., fcap. 8vo, 3s. 6d.

—— Goethe's Faust. Part II. Translated into English Verse. Second Edition, revised. Fcap. 8vo, 6s.

—— The Works of Horace. Translated into English Verse, with Life and Notes. 2 vols. New Edition, crown 8vo, 21s.

—— Poems and Ballads of Heinrich Heine. Done into English Verse. Second Edition. Printed on *papier vergé*, crown 8vo, 8s.

—— The Song of the Bell, and other Translations from Schiller, Goethe, Uhland, and Others. Crown 8vo, 7s. 6d.

—— Catullus. With Life and Notes. Second Ed., post 8vo, 7s. 6d.

—— Aladdin : A Dramatic Poem. By ADAM OEHLENSCHLAEGER. Fcap. 8vo, 5s.

—— Correggio : A Tragedy. By OEHLENSCHLAEGER. With Notes. Fcap. 8vo, 3s.

—— King Rene's Daughter : A Danish Lyrical Drama. By HENRIK HERTZ. Second Edition, fcap., 2s. 6d.

MARTIN. On some of Shakespeare's Female Characters. In a Series of Letters. By HELENA FAUCIT, LADY MARTIN. Dedicated by permission to Her Most Gracious Majesty the Queen. New Edition, enlarged. 8vo, with Portrait by Lane, 7s. 6d.

MATHESON. Can the Old Faith Live with the New? or the Problem of Evolution and Revelation. By the Rev. GEORGE MATHESON, D.D. Third Edition. Crown 8vo, 7s. 6d.

—— The Psalmist and the Scientist ; or, Modern Value of the Religious Sentiment. New and Cheaper Edition. Crown 8vo, 5s.

—— Spiritual Development of St Paul. Crown 8vo, 5s.

—— Sacred Songs. New and Cheaper Edition. Cr. 8vo, 2s. 6d.

MAURICE. The Balance of Military Power in Europe. An Examination of the War Resources of Great Britain and the Continental States. By Colonel MAURICE, R.A., Professor of Military Art and History at the Royal Staff College. Crown 8vo, with a Map. 6s

MEREDYTH. The Brief for the Government, 1886-92. A Handbook for Conservative and Unionist Writers, Speakers, &c. Second Edition. By W. H. MEREDYTH. Crown 8vo, 2s. 6d.

MICHEL. A Critical Inquiry into the Scottish Language. With the view of Illustrating the Rise and Progress of Civilisation in Scotland. By FRANCISQUE-MICHEL, F.S.A. Lond. and Scot., Correspondant de l'Institut de France, &c. 4to, printed on hand-made paper, and bound in Roxburghe, 66s.

MICHIE. The Larch : Being a Practical Treatise on its Culture and General Management. By CHRISTOPHER Y. MICHIE, Forester, Cullen House. Crown 8vo, with Illustrations. New and Cheaper Edition, enlarged, 5s.

—— The Practice of Forestry. Cr. 8vo, with Illustrations. 6s.

MIDDLETON. The Story of Alastair Bhan Comyn ; or, The Tragedy of Dunphail. A Tale of Tradition and Romance. By the Lady MIDDLETON. Square 8vo 10s. Cheaper Edition, 5s.

MILLER. Landscape Geology. A Plea for the Study of Geology by Landscape Painters. By HUGH MILLER, of H.M. Geological Survey. Cr. 8vo, 3s.

MILNE. The Problem of the Churchless and Poor in our Large Towns. With special reference to the Home Mission Work of the Church of Scotland. By the Rev. ROBT. MILNE, M.A., D.D., Ardler. New and Cheaper Edition. Crown 8vo, 1s.

MILNE-HOME.   Mamma's Black Nurse Stories.   West Indian
Folk-lore.   By MARY PAMELA MILNE-HOME.   With six full-page tinted Illustrations.   Small 4to, 5s.

MINTO.   A Manual of English Prose Literature, Biographical
and Critical : designed mainly to show Characteristics of Style.   By W. MINTO,
M.A., Professor of Logic in the University of Aberdeen.   Third Edition,
revised.   Crown 8vo, 7s. 6d.

—— Characteristics of English Poets, from Chaucer to Shirley.
New Edition, revised.   Crown 8vo, 7s. 6d.

MOIR.   Life of Mansie Wauch, Tailor in Dalkeith.   By D. M.
MOIR.   With 8 Illustrations on Steel, by the late GEORGE CRUIKSHANK.
Crown 8vo, 3s. 6d.   Another Edition, fcap. 8vo, 1s. 6d.

MOMERIE.   Defects of Modern Christianity, and other Sermons.
By ALFRED WILLIAMS MOMERIE, M.A., D.Sc., LL.D.   4th Edition.   Cr. 8vo, 5s.

—— The Basis of Religion.   Being an Examination of Natural
Religion.   Third Edition.   Crown 8vo, 2s. 6d.

—— The Origin of Evil, and other Sermons.   Seventh Edition,
enlarged.   Crown 8vo, 5s.

—— Personality.   The Beginning and End of Metaphysics, and
a Necessary Assumption in all Positive Philosophy.   Fourth Ed.   Cr. 8vo, 3s.

—— Agnosticism.   Third Edition, Revised.   Crown 8vo, 5s.

—— Preaching and Hearing ; and other Sermons.   Third
Edition, Enlarged.   Crown 8vo, 5s.

—— Belief in God.   Third Edition.   Crown 8vo, 3s.

—— Inspiration ; and other Sermons.   Second Ed.   Cr. 8vo, 5s.

—— Church and Creed.   Second Edition.   Crown 8vo, 4s. 6d.

MONTAGUE.   Campaigning in South Africa.   Reminiscences of
an Officer in 1879.   By Captain W. E. MONTAGUE, 94th Regiment, Author of
' Claude Meadowleigh,' &c.   8vo, 10s. 6d.

MONTALEMBERT.   Memoir of Count de Montalembert.   A
Chapter of Recent French History.   By Mrs OLIPHANT, Author of the ' Life
of Edward Irving,' &c.   2 vols. crown 8vo, £1, 4s.

MORISON.   Sordello.   An Outline Analysis of Mr Browning's
Poem.   By JEANIE MORISON, Author of ' The Purpose of the Ages,' ' Ane
Booke of Ballades,' &c.   Crown 8vo, 3s.

—— Selections from Poems.   Crown 8vo, 4s. 6d.

—— There as Here.   Crown 8vo, 3s.
₊ A limited impression on handmade paper, bound in vellum, 7s. 6d.

MUNRO.   On Valuation of Property.   By WILLIAM MUNRO, M.A.,
Her Majesty's Assessor of Railways and Canals for Scotland.   Second Edition.
Revised and enlarged.   8vo, 3s. 6d.

MURDOCH.   Manual of the Law of Insolvency and Bankruptcy :
Comprehending a Summary of the Law of Insolvency, Notour Bankruptcy,
Composition - contracts, Trust-deeds, Cessios, and Sequestrations ; and the
Winding-up of Joint-Stock Companies in Scotland ; with Annotations on the
various Insolvency and Bankruptcy Statutes ; and with Forms of Procedure
applicable to these Subjects.   By JAMES MURDOCH, Member of the Faculty of
Procurators in Glasgow.   Fifth Edition, Revised and Enlarged, 8vo, £1, 10s.

MY TRIVIAL LIFE AND MISFORTUNE : A Gossip with
no Plot in Particular.   By A PLAIN WOMAN.   Cheap Ed., crown 8vo, 3s. 6d.
                          By the SAME AUTHOR.
        POOR NELLIE.   New Edition.   Crown 8vo, 6s.

NAPIER.   The Construction of the Wonderful Canon of Logar-
ithms (Mirifici Logarithmorum Canonis Constructio).   By JOHN NAPIER of
Merchiston.   Translated for the first time, with Notes, and a Catalogue of
Napier's Works, by WILLIAM RAE MACDONALD.   Small 4to, 15s.   *A few large
paper copies may be had, printed on Whatman paper, price* 30s.

NEAVES. Songs and Verses, Social and Scientific. By an Old
Contributor to 'Maga.' By the Hon. Lord NEAVES. Fifth Ed., fcap. 8vo, 4s.

—— The Greek Anthology. Being Vol. XX. of 'Ancient
Classics for English Readers.' Crown 8vo, 2s. 6d.

NICHOLSON. A Manual of Zoology, for the Use of Students.
With a General Introduction on the Principles of Zoology. By HENRY AL-
LEYNE NICHOLSON, M.D., D.Sc., F.L.S., F.G.S., Regius Professor of Natural
History in the University of Aberdeen. Seventh Edition, rewritten and
enlarged. Post 8vo, pp. 956, with 555 Engravings on Wood, 18s.

—— Text-Book of Zoology, for the Use of Schools. Fourth Edition, enlarged. Crown 8vo, with 188 Engravings on Wood, 7s. 6d.

—— Introductory Text-Book of Zoology, for the Use of Junior
Classes. Sixth Edition, revised and enlarged, with 166 Engravings, 3s.

—— Outlines of Natural History, for Beginners ; being Descriptions of a Progressive Series of Zoological Types. Third Edition, with
Engravings, 1s. 6d.

—— A Manual of Palæontology, for the Use of Students.
With a General Introduction on the Principles of Palæontology. By Professor
H. ALLEYNE NICHOLSON and RICHARD LYDEKKER, B.A. Third Edition. Re-
written and greatly enlarged. 2 vols. 8vo, with Engravings, £3, 3s.

—— The Ancient Life-History of the Earth. An Outline of
the Principles and Leading Facts of Palæontological Science. Crown 8vo,
with 276 Engravings, 10s. 6d.

—— On the "Tabulate Corals" of the Palæozoic Period, with
Critical Descriptions of Illustrative Species. Illustrated with 15 Litho-
graph Plates and numerous Engravings. Super-royal 8vo, 21s.

—— Synopsis of the Classification of the Animal Kingdom. 8vo, with 106 Illustrations, 6s.

—— On the Structure and Affinities of the Genus Monticuli-
pora and its Sub-Genera, with Critical Descriptions of Illustrative Species.
Illustrated with numerous Engravings on wood and lithographed Plates.
Super-royal 8vo, 18s.

NICHOLSON. Communion with Heaven, and other Sermons.
By the late MAXWELL NICHOLSON, D.D., Minister of St Stephen's, Edinburgh.
Crown 8vo, 5s. 6d.

—— Rest in Jesus. Sixth Edition. Fcap. 8vo, 4s. 6d.

NICHOLSON. A Treatise on Money, and Essays on Present
Monetary Problems. By JOSEPH SHIELD NICHOLSON, M.A., D.Sc., Professor
of Commercial and Political Economy and Mercantile Law in the University
of Edinburgh. 8vo, 10s. 6d.

—— Thoth. A Romance. Third Edition. Crown 8vo, 4s. 6d.

—— A Dreamer of Dreams. A Modern Romance. Second
Edition. Crown 8vo, 6s.

NICOLSON AND MURE. A Handbook to the Local Govern-
ment (Scotland) Act, 1889. With Introduction, Explanatory Notes, and
Index. By J. BADENACH NICOLSON, Advocate, Counsel to the Scotch Education Department, and W. J. MURE, Advocate, Legal Secretary to the Lord
Advocate for Scotland. Ninth Reprint. 8vo, 5s.

OLIPHANT. Masollam : a Problem of the Period. A Novel.
By LAURENCE OLIPHANT. 3 vols. post 8vo, 25s. 6d.

—— Scientific Religion ; or, Higher Possibilities of Life and
Practice through the Operation of Natural Forces. Second Edition. 8vo, 16s.

—— Altiora Peto. By LAURENCE OLIPHANT. Cheap Edition.
Crown 8vo, boards, 2s. 6d.; cloth, 3s. 6d. Illustrated Edition. Crown 8vo,
cloth, 6s.

—— Piccadilly: A Fragment of Contemporary Biography.
With Illustrations by Richard Doyle. New Edition, 3s. 6d. Cheap
Edition, boards, 2s. 6d.

—— Traits and Travesties ; Social and Political. Post 8vo, 10s. 6d.

OLIPHANT.   The Land of Gilead.   With Excursions in the
Lebanon.   With Illustrations and Maps.   Demy 8vo, 21s.
——— Haifa : Life in Modern Palestine. 2d Edition. 8vo, 7s. 6d.
——— Episodes in a Life of Adventure ; or, Moss from a Rolling
Rolling Stone.   Fifth Edition.   Post 8vo, 6s.
——— Memoir of the Life of Laurence Oliphant, and of Alice
Oliphant, his Wife.   By Mrs M. O. W. OLIPHANT.   Seventh Edition.   In 2 vols.
post 8vo, with Portraits.   21s.
OLIPHANT.   Katie Stewart.   By Mrs OLIPHANT.   2s. 6d.
——— The Duke's Daughter, and The Fugitives. A Novel. 3 vols.
crown 8vo, 25s. 6d.
——— Two Stories of the Seen and the Unseen.   The Open Door
—Old Lady Mary.   Paper Covers, 1s.
——— Sons and Daughters.   Crown 8vo, 3s. 6d.
OLIPHANT.   Notes of a Pilgrimage to Jerusalem and the Holy
Land.   By F. R. OLIPHANT.   Crown 8vo, 3s. 6d.
ON SURREY HILLS.   By "A SON OF THE MARSHES." Cr. 8vo, 6s.
OSBORN.   Narratives of Voyage and Adventure.   By Admiral
SHERARD OSBORN, C.B.   3 vols. crown 8vo, 12s.
OSSIAN.   The Poems of Ossian in the Original Gaelic.   With a
Literal Translation into English, and a Dissertation on the Authenticity of the
Poems.   By the Rev. ARCHIBALD CLERK.   2 vols. imperial 8vo, £1, 11s. 6d.
OSWALD.   By Fell and Fjord ; or, Scenes and Studies in Iceland.
By E. J. OSWALD.   Post 8vo, with Illustrations.   7s. 6d.
OWEN.   Annals of a Fishing Village.   Drawn from the Notes of
"A Son of the Marshes."   Edited by J. A. OWEN.   Crown 8vo, with Illustra-
tions, 7s. 6d.
PAGE.   Introductory Text-Book of Geology.   By DAVID PAGE,
LL.D., Professor of Geology in the Durham University of Physical Science
Newcastle, and Professor LAPWORTH of Mason Science College, Birmingham.
With Engravings and Glossarial Index.   Twelfth Edition.   Revised and En-
larged.   3s. 6d.
——— Advanced Text-Book of Geology, Descriptive and Indus-
trial.   With Engravings, and Glossary of Scientific Terms.   Sixth Edition, re-
vised and enlarged, 7s. 6d.
——— Introductory Text-Book of Physical Geography.   With
Sketch-Maps and Illustrations. Edited by CHARLES LAPWORTH, LL.D., F.G.S.,
&c., Professor of Geology and Mineralogy in the Mason Science College, Bir-
mingham.   12th Edition.   2s. 6d.
——— Advanced Text-Book of Physical Geography.   Third
Edition, Revised and Enlarged by Prof. LAPWORTH.   With Engravings.   5s.
PATON.   Spindrift.   By Sir J. NOEL PATON.   Fcap., cloth, 5s.
——— Poems by a Painter.   Fcap., cloth, 5s.
PATON.   Body and Soul.   A Romance in Transcendental Path-
ology.   By FREDERICK NOEL PATON.   Third Edition.   Crown 8vo, 1s.
PATTERSON.   Essays in History and Art.   By R. HOGARTH
PATTERSON.   8vo, 12s.
——— The New Golden Age, and Influence of the Precious
Metals upon the World.   2 vols. 8vo, 31s. 6d.
PAUL.   History of the Royal Company of Archers, the Queen's
Body-Guard for Scotland.   By JAMES BALFOUR PAUL, Advocate of the Scottish
Bar.   Crown 4to, with Portraits and other Illustrations.   £2, 2s.
PEILE.   Lawn Tennis as a Game of Skill.   With latest revised
Laws as played by the Best Clubs.   By Captain S. C. F. PEILE, B.S.C.   Cheaper
Edition, fcap. cloth, 1s.
PETTIGREW.   The Handy Book of Bees, and their Profitable
Management.   By A. PETTIGREW.   Fifth Edition, Enlarged, with Engrav-
ings.   Crown 8vo, 3s. 6d.

PHILOSOPHICAL CLASSICS FOR ENGLISH READERS.
Edited by WILLIAM KNIGHT, LL.D., Professor of Moral Philosophy, University of St Andrews. In crown 8vo volumes, with portraits, price 3s. 6d.
[For list of Volumes published, see page 2.

PHILIP. The Function of Labour in the Production of Wealth.
By ALEXANDER PHILIP, LL.B., Edinburgh. Crown 8vo, 3s. 6d

POLLOK. The Course of Time : A Poem. By ROBERT POLLOK,
A.M. Small fcap. 8vo, cloth gilt, 2s. 6d. Cottage Edition, 32mo, 8d. The
Same, cloth, gilt edges, 1s. 6d. Another Edition, with Illustrations by Birket
Foster and others, fcap., cloth, 3s. 6d., or with edges gilt, 4s.

PORT ROYAL LOGIC. Translated from the French ; with Introduction, Notes, and Appendix. By THOMAS SPENCER BAYNES, LL.D., Professor in the University of St Andrews. Tenth Edition, 12mo, 4s.

POTTS AND DARNELL. Aditus Faciliores : An easy Latin Construing Book, with Complete Vocabulary. By the late A. W. POTTS, M.A.,
LL.D., and the Rev. C. DARNELL, M.A., Head-Master of Cargilfield Prepara-
tory School, Edinburgh. Tenth Edition, fcap. 8vo, 3s. 6d.

——— Aditus Faciliores Graeci. An easy Greek Construing Book,
with Complete Vocabulary. Fourth Edition, fcap. 8vo, 3s.

POTTS. School Sermons. By the late ALEXANDER WM. POTTS,
LL.D., First Head-Master of Fettes College. With a Memoir and Portrait.
Crown 8vo, 7s. 6d.

PRINGLE. The Live-Stock of the Farm. By ROBERT O. PRINGLE.
Third Edition. Revised and Edited by JAMES MACDONALD. Cr. 8vo, 7s. 6d.

PUBLIC GENERAL STATUTES AFFECTING SCOTLAND
from 1707 to 1847, with Chronological Table and Index. 3 vols. large 8vo, £3, 3s.

PUBLIC GENERAL STATUTES AFFECTING SCOTLAND,
COLLECTION OF. Published Annually with General Index.

RADICAL CURE FOR IRELAND, The. A Letter to the People
of England and Scotland concerning a new Plantation. With 2 Maps. 8vo, 7s. 6d.

RAMSAY. Rough Recollections of Military Service and Society.
By Lieut.-Col. BALCARRES D. WARDLAW RAMSAY. Two vols. post 8vo, 21s.

RAMSAY. Scotland and Scotsmen in the Eighteenth Century.
Edited from the MSS. of JOHN RAMSAY, Esq. of Ochtertyre, by ALEXANDER
ALLARDYCE, Author of 'Memoir of Admiral Lord Keith, K.B.,' &c. 2 vols.
8vo, 31s. 6d.

RANKIN. A Handbook of the Church of Scotland. By JAMES
RANKIN, D.D., Minister of Muthill; Author of 'Character Studies in the
Old Testament,' &c. An entirely New and much Enlarged Edition. Crown
8vo, with 2 Maps, 7s. 6d.

——— The Creed in Scotland. An Exposition of the Apostles'
Creed. With Extracts from Archbishop Hamilton's Catechism of 1552, John
Calvin's Catechism of 1556, and a Catena of Ancient Latin and other Hymns.
Post 8vo, 7s. 6d.

——— First Communion Lessons. Twenty-third Edition. Paper
Cover, 2d.

RECORDS OF THE TERCENTENARY FESTIVAL OF THE
UNIVERSITY OF EDINBURGH. Celebrated in April 1884. Published
under the Sanction of the Senatus Academicus. Large 4to, £2, 12s. 6d.

ROBERTSON. Early Religion of Israel. Being the Baird Lecture for 1888-89. By JAMES ROBERTSON, D.D., Professor of Oriental Languages in the University of Glasgow. In one Vol. crown 8vo. [Immediately.

ROBERTSON. Orellana, and other Poems. By J. LOGIE ROBERT-
SON. M.A. Fcap. 8vo. Printed on hand-made paper. 6s.

ROBERTSON. Our Holiday Among the Hills. By JAMES and
JANET LOGIE ROBERTSON. Fcap. 8vo, 3s. 6d.

ROSCOE. Rambles with a Fishing-rod. By E. S. ROSCOE. Crown
8vo, 4s. 6d.

ROSS. Old Scottish Regimental Colours. By ANDREW ROSS,
S.S.C., Hon. Secretary Old Scottish Regimental Colours Committee. Dedicated by Special Permission to Her Majesty the Queen. Folio. £2, 12s. 6d.

RUSSELL. The Haigs of Bemersyde. A Family History. By JOHN RUSSELL. Large 8vo, with Illustrations. 21s.

RUSSELL. Fragments from Many Tables. Being the Recollections of some Wise and Witty Men and Women. By GEO. RUSSELL. Cr. 8vo, 4s. 6d.

RUTLAND. Notes of an Irish Tour in 1846. By the DUKE OF RUTLAND, G.C.B. (Lord JOHN MANNERS). New Edition. Crown 8vo, 2s. 6d.

——— Correspondence between the Right Honble. William Pitt and Charles Duke of Rutland, Lord Lieutenant of Ireland, 1781-1787. With Introductory Note by John Duke of Rutland. 8vo, 7s. 6d.

RUTLAND. Gems of German Poetry. Translated by the DUCHESS OF RUTLAND (Lady JOHN MANNERS). [New Edition in preparation.

——— Impressions of Bad-Homburg. Comprising a Short Account of the Women's Associations of Germany under the Red Cross. Crown 8vo, 1s. 6d.

——— Some Personal Recollections of the Later Years of the Earl of Beaconsfield, K.G. Sixth Edition, 6d.

——— Employment of Women in the Public Service. 6d.

——— Some of the Advantages of Easily Accessible Reading and Recreation Rooms, and Free Libraries. With Remarks on Starting and Maintaining Them. Second Edition, crown 8vo, 1s.

——— A Sequel to Rich Men's Dwellings, and other Occasional Papers. Crown 8vo, 2s. 6d.

——— Encouraging Experiences of Reading and Recreation Rooms, Aims of Guilds, Nottingham Social Guild, Existing Institutions, &c., &c. Crown 8vo, 1s.

SCHILLER. Wallenstein. A Dramatic Poem. By FREDERICK VON SCHILLER. Translated by C. G. A. LOCKHART. Fcap. 8vo, 7s. 6d.

SCOTCH LOCH FISHING. By "Black Palmer." Crown 8vo, interleaved with blank pages, 4s.

SCOUGAL. Prisons and their Inmates; or, Scenes from a Silent World. By FRANCIS SCOUGAL. Crown 8vo, boards, 2s.

SELLAR. Manual of the Education Acts for Scotland. By the late ALEXANDER CRAIG SELLAR, M.P. Eighth Edition. Revised and in great part rewritten by J. EDWARD GRAHAM, B.A. Oxon., Advocate. With Rules for the conduct of Elections. with Notes and Cases. With a Supplement, being the Acts of 1889 in so far as affecting the Education Acts. 8vo, 12s. 6d.
[SUPPLEMENT TO SELLAR'S MANUAL OF THE EDUCATION ACTS. 8vo, 2s.]

SETH. Scottish Philosophy. A Comparison of the Scottish and German Answers to Hume. Balfour Philosophical Lectures, University of Edinburgh. By ANDREW SETH, M.A., Professor of Logic and Metaphysics in Edinburgh University. Second Edition. Crown 8vo, 5s.

——— Hegelianism and Personality. Balfour Philosophical Lectures. Second Series. Crown 8vo, 5s.

SETH. Freedom as Ethical Postulate. By JAMES SETH, M.A., George Munro Professor of Philosophy, Dalhousie College, Halifax, Canada. 8vo, 1s.

SHADWELL. The Life of Colin Campbell, Lord Clyde. Illustrated by Extracts from his Diary and Correspondence. By Lieutenant-General SHADWELL, C.B. 2 vols. 8vo. With Portrait, Maps, and Plans. 36s.

SHAND. Half a Century; or, Changes in Men and Manners. By ALEX. INNES SHAND, Author of 'Against Time,' &c. Second Edition, 8vo, 12s. 6d.

——— Letters from the West of Ireland. Reprinted from the 'Times.' Crown 8vo. 5s.

——— Kilcarra. A Novel. 3 vols. crown 8vo, 25s. 6d.

SHARPE. Letters from and to Charles Kirkpatrick Sharpe. Edited by ALEXANDER ALLARDYCE, Author of 'Memoir of Admiral Lord Keith, K.B.,' &c With a Memoir by the Rev. W. K. R. BEDFORD. In two vols. 8vo. Illustrated with Etchings and other Engravings. £2, 12s. 6d.

SIM. Margaret Sim's Cookery. With. an Introduction by L. B. WALFORD, Author of 'Mr Smith : A Part of His Life,' &c. Crown 8vo, 5s.

SKELTON. Maitland of Lethington ; and the Scotland of Mary Stuart. A History. By JOHN SKELTON, C.B., LL.D., Author of 'The Essays of Shirley.' Demy 8vo. 2 vols., 28s.

—— The Handbook of Public Health. A Complete Edition of the Public Health and other Sanitary Acts relating to Scotland. Annotated, and with the Rules, Instructions, and Decisions of the Board of Supervision brought up to date with relative forms. 8vo, with Supplement, 8s. 6d.

—— Supplement to Skelton's Handbook. The Administration of the Public Health Act in Counties. 8vo, cloth, 1s.

—— The Local Government (Scotland) Act in Relation to Public Health. A Handy Guide for County and District Councillors, Medical Officers, Sanitary Inspectors, and Members of Parochial Boards. Second Edition. With a new Preface on appointment of Sanitary Officers. Crown 8vo, 2s.

SMITH. For God and Humanity. A Romance of Mount Carmel. By HASKETT SMITH, Author of 'The Divine Epiphany,' &c. 3 vols. post 8vo, 25s. 6d.

SMITH. Thorndale ; or, The Conflict of Opinions. By WILLIAM SMITH, Author of 'A Discourse on Ethics,' &c. New Edition. Cr. 8vo. 10s. 6d.

—— Gravenhurst ; or, Thoughts on Good and Evil. Second Edition, with Memoir of the Author. Crown 8vo, 8s.

—— The Story of William and Lucy Smith. Edited by GEORGE MERRIAM. Large post 8vo, 12s. 6d.

SMITH. Memoir of the Families of M'Combie and Thoms, originally M'Intosh and M'Thomas. Compiled from History and Tradition. By WILLIAM M'COMBIE SMITH. With Illustrations. 8vo, 7s. 6d.

SMITH. Greek Testament Lessons for Colleges, Schools, and Private Students, consisting chiefly of the Sermon on the Mount and the Parables of our Lord. With Notes and Essays. By the Rev. J. HUNTER SMITH, M.A., King Edward's School, Birmingham. Crown 8vo, 6s.

SMITH. Writings by the Way. By JOHN CAMPBELL SMITH, M.A., Sheriff-Substitute. Crown 8vo, 9s.

SMITH. The Secretary for Scotland. Being a Statement of the Powers and Duties of the new Scottish Office. With a Short Historical Introduction and numerous references to important Administrative Documents. By W. C. SMITH, LL. B., Advocate. 8vo, 6s.

SORLEY. The Ethics of Naturalism. Being the Shaw Fellowship Lectures, 1884. By W. R. SORLEY, M.A., Fellow of Trinity College, Cambridge, Professor of Logic and Philosophy in University College of South Wales. Crown 8vo, 6s.

SPEEDY. Sport in the Highlands and Lowlands of Scotland with Rod and Gun. By TOM SPEEDY. Second Edition, Revised and Enlarged. With Illustrations by Lieut.-Gen. Hope Crealocke, C.B., C.M.G., and others. 8vo, 15s.

SPROTT. The Worship and Offices of the Church of Scotland. By GEORGE W. SPROTT. D.D., Minister of North Berwick. Crown 8vo, 6s.

STAFFORD. How I Spent my Twentieth Year. Being a Record of a Tour Round the World, 1886-87. By the MARCHIONESS OF STAFFORD. With Illustrations. Third Edition, crown 8vo, 8s. 6d.

STARFORTH. Villa Residences and Farm Architecture : A Series of Designs. By JOHN STARFORTH, Architect. 102 Engravings. Second Edition, medium 4to, £2, 17s. 6d.

STATISTICAL ACCOUNT OF SCOTLAND. Complete, with Index, 15 vols. 8vo, £16, 16s. Each County sold separately, with Title, Index, and Map, neatly bound in cloth.

STEPHENS' BOOK OF THE FARM ; detailing the Labours of the Farmer, Farm-Steward, Ploughman, Shepherd, Hedger, Farm-Labourer, Field-Worker, and Cattleman. Illustrated with numerous Portraits of Animals and Engravings of Implements, and Plans of Farm Buildings. Fourth Edition. Revised, and in great part rewritten by JAMES MACDONALD, of the 'Farming World,' &c., &c. Assisted by many of the leading agricultural authorities of the day. Complete in Six Divisional Volumes. bound in cloth, each 10s. 6d., or handsomely bound, in 3 volumes, with leather back and gilt

STEPHENS. The Book of Farm Implements and Machines. By
J. SLIGHT and R. SCOTT BURN, Engineers. Edited by HENRY STEPHENS. Large
8vo, £2, 2s.

STEVENSON. British Fungi. (Hymenomycetes.) By Rev. JOHN
STEVENSON, Author of 'Mycologia Scotia,' Hon. Sec. Cryptogamic Society of
Scotland. 2 vols. post 8vo, with Illustrations, price 12s. 6d. each.
Vol. I. AGARICUS—BOLBITIUS. Vol. II. CORTINARIUS—DACRYMYCES.

STEWART. Advice to Purchasers of Horses. By JOHN STEWART,
V.S. New Edition. 2s. 6d.

—— Stable Economy. A Treatise on the Management of
Horses in relation to Stabling, Grooming, Feeding, Watering, and Working.
Seventh Edition, fcap. 8vo, 6s. 6d.

STEWART. A Hebrew Grammar, with the Pronunciation, Syl-
labic Division and Tone of the Words, and Quantity of the Vowels. By Rev.
DUNCAN STEWART, D.D. Fourth Edition. 8vo, 3s. 6d.

STEWART. Boethius : An Essay. By HUGH FRASER STEWART,
M.A., Trinity College, Cambridge. Crown 8vo, 7s. 6d.

STODDART. Angling Songs. By THOMAS TOD STODDART. New
Edition, with a Memoir by ANNA M. STODDART. Crown 8vo, 7s. 6d.

STORMONTH. Etymological and Pronouncing Dictionary of the
English Language. Including a very Copious Selection of Scientific Terms
For Use in Schools and Colleges, and as a Book of General Reference. By the
Rev. JAMES STORMONTH. The Pronunciation carefully Revised by the Rev.
P. H. PHELP, M.A. Cantab. Tenth Edition, Revised throughout. Crown
8vo, pp. 800. 7s. 6d.

—— Dictionary of the English Language, Pronouncing,
Etymological, and Explanatory. Revised by the Rev. P. H. PHELP. Library
Edition. Imperial 8vo, handsomely bound in half morocco, 31s. 6d.

—— The School Etymological Dictionary and Word-Book.
Fourth Edition. Fcap. 8vo, pp. 254. 2s.

STORY. Nero ; A Historical Play. By W. W. STORY, Author of
'Roba di Roma.' Fcap. 8vo, 6s.

—— Vallombrosa. Post 8vo, 5s.

—— Poems. 2 vols. fcap., 7s. 6d.

—— Fiammetta. A Summer Idyl. Crown 8vo, 7s. 6d.

—— Conversations in a Studio. 2 vols. crown 8vo, 12s. 6d.

—— Excursions in Art and Letters. Crown 8vo, 7s. 6d.

STRICKLAND. Life of Agnes Strickland. By her SISTER.
Post 8vo, with Portrait engraved on Steel, 12s. 6d.

STURGIS. John-a-Dreams. A Tale. By JULIAN STURGIS.
New Edition, crown 8vo, 3s. 6d.

—— Little Comedies, Old and New. Crown 8vo, 7s. 6d.

SUTHERLAND. Handbook of Hardy Herbaceous and Alpine
Flowers, for general Garden Decoration. Containing Descriptions of up-
wards of 1000 Species of Ornamental Hardy Perennial and Alpine Plants;
along with Concise and Plain Instructions for their Propagation and Culture.
By WILLIAM SUTHERLAND, Landscape Gardener ; formerly Manager of the
Herbaceous Department at Kew. Crown 8vo, 7s. 6d.

TAYLOR. The Story of My Life. By the late Colonel MEADOWS
TAYLOR, Author of 'The Confessions of a Thug,' &c. &c. Edited by his
Daughter. New and cheaper Edition, being the Fourth. Crown 8vo, 6s.

THOLUCK. Hours of Christian Devotion. Translated from the
German of A. Tholuck, D.D., Professor of Theology in the University of Halle.
By the Rev. ROBERT MENZIES, D.D. With a Preface written for this Transla-
tion by the Author. Second Edition, crown 8vo, 7s. 6d.

THOMSON. Handy Book of the Flower-Garden : being Practical
Directions for the Propagation, Culture, and Arrangement of Plants in Flower-
Gardens all the year round. With Engraved Plans. By DAVID THOMSON,
Gardener to his Grace the Duke of Buccleuch, K.T., at Drumlanrig. Fourth
and Cheaper Edition, crown 8vo, 5s.

THOMSON. The Handy Book of Fruit-Culture under Glass: being a series of Elaborate Practical Treatises on the Cultivation and Forcing of Pines, Vines, Peaches, Figs, Melons, Strawberries, and Cucumbers. With Engravings of Hothouses, &c. Second Ed. Cr. 8vo, 7s. 6d.

THOMSON. A Practical Treatise on the Cultivation of the Grape Vine. By WILLIAM THOMSON, Tweed Vineyards. Tenth Edition, 8vo, 5s.

THOMSON. Cookery for the Sick and Convalescent. With Directions for the Preparation of Poultices, Fomentations, &c. By BARBARA THOMSON. Fcap. 8vo, 1s. 6d.

THORNTON. Opposites. A Series of Essays on the Unpopular Sides of Popular Questions. By LEWIS THORNTON. 8vo, 12s. 6d.

TOM CRINGLE'S LOG. A New Edition, with Illustrations. Crown 8vo, cloth gilt, 5s. Cheap Edition, 2s.

TRANSACTIONS OF THE HIGHLAND AND AGRICUL-TURAL SOCIETY OF SCOTLAND. Published annually, price 5s.

TULLOCH. Rational Theology and Christian Philosophy in England in the Seventeenth Century. By JOHN TULLOCH, D.D., Principal of St Mary's College in the University of St Andrews; and one of her Majesty's Chaplains in Ordinary in Scotland. Second Edition. 2 vols. 8vo, 16s.

—— Modern Theories in Philosophy and Religion. 8vo, 15s.

—— Luther, and other Leaders of the Reformation. Third Edition, enlarged. Crown 8vo, 3s. 6d.

—— Memoir of Principal Tulloch, D.D., LL.D. By Mrs OLIPHANT, Author of 'Life of Edward Irving.' Third and Cheaper Edition. 8vo, with Portrait. 7s. 6d.

TWEEDIE. The Arabian Horse: his Country and People. With Portraits of Typical or Famous Arabians, and numerous other Illustrations; also a Map of the Country of the Arabian Horse, and a descriptive Glossary of Arabic words and proper names. By Colonel W. TWEEDIE, C.S.I., Bengal Staff Corps, H.B M.'s late Consul-General, Baghdad. [In the press.

VEITCH. Institutes of Logic. By JOHN VEITCH, LL.D., Professor of Logic and Rhetoric in the University of Glasgow. Post 8vo, 12s. 6d

—— The Feeling for Nature in Scottish Poetry. From the Earliest Times to the Present Day. 2 vols. fcap. 8vo, in roxburghe binding. 15s.

—— Merlin and Other Poems. Fcap. 8vo. 4s. 6d.

—— Knowing and Being. Essays in Philosophy. First Series. Crown 8vo, 5s.

VIRGIL. The Æneid of Virgil. Translated in English Blank Verse by G. K. RICKARDS, M.A., and Lord RAVENSWORTH. 2 vols. fcap. 8vo, 10s.

WALFORD. Four Biographies from 'Blackwood': Jane Taylor, Hannah More, Elizabeth Fry, Mary Somerville. By L. B. WALFORD. Crown 8vo, 5s.

WARREN'S (SAMUEL) WORKS :—
Diary of a Late Physician. Cloth, 2s. 6d.; boards, 2s.
Ten Thousand A-Year. Cloth, 3s. 6d.; boards, 2s. 6d.
Now and Then. The Lily and the Bee. Intellectual and Moral Development of the Present Age. 4s. 6d.
Essays : Critical, Imaginative, and Juridical. 5s.

WARREN. The Five Books of the Psalms. With Marginal Notes. By Rev. SAMUEL L. WARREN, Rector of Esher, Surrey; late Fellow, Dean, and Divinity Lecturer, Wadham College, Oxford. Crown 8vo, 5s.

WEBSTER. The Angler and the Loop-Rod. By DAVID WEBSTER. Crown 8vo, with Illustrations, 7s. 6d.

WELLINGTON. Wellington Prize Essays on "the System of Field Manoeuvres best adapted for enabling our Troops to meet a Continental Army." Edited by General Sir EDWARD BRUCE HAMLEY, K.C.B., K.C.M.G. 8vo, 12s. 6d.

WENLEY. Socrates and Christ: A Study in the Philosophy of
Religion. By R. M. WENLEY, M.A., Lecturer on Mental and Moral Philoso-
phy in Queen Margaret College, Glasgow; Examiner in Philosophy in the
University of Glasgow. Crown 8vo, 6s.

WERNER. A Visit to Stanley's Rear-Guard at Major Bartte-
lot's Camp on the Aruhwimi. With an Account of River-Life on the Congo.
By J. R. WERNER, F.R.G.S., Engineer, late in the Service of the Etat Inde-
pendant du Congo. With Maps, Portraits, and other Illustrations. 8vo. 16s.

WESTMINSTER ASSEMBLY. Minutes of the Westminster As-
sembly, while engaged in preparing their Directory for Church Government,
Confession of Faith, and Catechisms (November 1644 to March 1649). Edited
by the Rev. Professor ALEX. T. MITCHELL, of St Andrews, and the Rev. JOHN
STRUTHERS, LL.D. With a Historical and Critical Introduction by Professor
Mitchell. 8vo, 15s.

WHITE. The Eighteen Christian Centuries. By the Rev. JAMES
WHITE. Seventh Edition, post 8vo, with Index, 6s.

—— History of France, from the Earliest Times. Sixth Thousand, post 8vo, with Index, 6s.

WHITE. Archæological Sketches in Scotland—Kintyre and Knap-
dale. By Colonel T. P. WHITE, R.E., of the Ordnance Survey. With numerous
Illustrations. 2 vols. folio, £4, 4s. Vol. I., Kintyre, sold separately, £2, 2s.

—— The Ordnance Survey of the United Kingdom. A Popular
Account. Crown 8vo, 5s.

WICKS. Golden Lives. The Story of a Woman's Courage. By
FREDERICK WICKS. Cheap Edition, with 120 Illustrations. Illustrated
Boards. 8vo, 2s. 6d.

WILLIAMSON. Poems of Nature and Life. By DAVID R.
WILLIAMSON, Minister of Kirkmaiden. Fcap. 8vo, 3s.

WILLS AND GREENE. Drawing-room Dramas for Children. By
W. G. WILLS and the Hon. Mrs GREENE. Crown 8vo, 6s.

WILSON. Works of Professor Wilson. Edited by his Son-in-Law,
Professor FERRIER. 12 vols. crown 8vo, £2, 8s.

—— Christopher in his Sporting-Jacket. 2 vols., 8s.

—— Isle of Palms, City of the Plague, and other Poems. 4s.

—— Lights and Shadows of Scottish Life, and other Tales. 4s.

—— Essays, Critical and Imaginative. 4 vols., 16s.

—— The Noctes Ambrosianæ. 4 vols., 16s.

—— Homer and his Translators, and the Greek Drama. Crown
8vo, 4s.

WINGATE. Lily Neil. A Poem. By DAVID WINGATE. Crown
8vo, 4s. 6d.

WORDSWORTH. The Historical Plays of Shakspeare. With
Introductions and Notes. By CHARLES WORDSWORTH, D.C.L., Bishop of S.
Andrews. 3 vols. post 8vo, cloth, each price 7s. 6d., or handsomely bound in
half-calf, each price 9s. 9d.

WORSLEY. Poems and Translations. By PHILIP STANHOPE
WORSLEY, M.A. Edited by EDWARD WORSLEY. 2d Ed., enlarged. Fcap. 8vo, 6s.

YATE. England and Russia Face to Face in Asia. A Record of
Travel with the Afghan Boundary Commission. By Captain A. C. YATE
Bombay Staff Corps. 8vo, with Maps and Illustrations, 21s.

YATE. Northern Afghanistan; or, Letters from the Afghan
Boundary Commission. By Major C. E. YATE, C.S.I., C.M.G. Bombay Staff
Corps, F.R.G.S. 8vo, with Maps. 18s.

YOUNG. A Story of Active Service in Foreign Lands. Compiled
from letters sent home from South Africa, India, and China, 1856-1882. By
Surgeon-General A. GRAHAM YOUNG, Author of 'Crimean Cracks.' Crown
8vo, Illustrated, 7s. 6d.

YULE. Fortification: for the Use of Officers in the Army, and
Readers of Military History. By Col. YULE, Bengal Engineers. 8vo, with
numerous Illustrations, 10s. 6d.

www.ingramcontent.com/pod-product-compliance
Lightning Source LLC
Chambersburg PA
CBHW030836270326
41928CB00007B/1076